ABOUT THIS BOOK

The College Experience is not like most books. It stands out from other self-help books in an important way. It's not a book to read—it's book to *use.* The unique week-by-week self-paced format and the many worksheets encourage the reader to apply what is learned on a day-by-day basis in making her or his successful transition into a new environment.

The objective of *The College Experience* is to help you make a successful adjustment to academic and college life. Using this book is a win-win situation—you will get off to a better start and substantially reduce your chances of becoming a discouraged dropout.

The College Experience (and other titles listed in the back of this book) can be used effectively in a number of ways. Here are some possibilities:

Orientation Programs: *The College Experience* is ideal for all orientation programs regardless of length.

- The book is short, lively, and appropriate for all students.
- The cost has purposely been kept low.
- The book refers students to campus support groups as well as other publications.
- Materials developed locally can be used to supplement the book.

Individual Study: Where formal orientation programs are not available, *The College Experience* can be made available in various ways:

- It can be sold during registration.
- It can be required for all students or for specified students, depending upon local circumstances.
- It can be recommended by guidance staff.

Prearrival: *The College Experience* is also designed for those who wish to prepare at home before reporting on campus.

There are several other possibilities that depend on the objectives, orientation program, or ideas of the college.

One thing for sure: even after it has been read, this book will be looked at—and thought about—again and again.

WHY THIRTY DAYS?

There are many reasons why a practical, thirty-day college orientation program makes sense.

- Thirty days is long enough to show yourself and your peers that you can survive college with style and be on your way to academic success.
- Thirty days is not so long that people become discouraged and give up. You can keep a clear focus on your goal and reward yourself for reaching it.
- Behavioral changes are usually achieved only after a strong commitment is made. People are more apt to commit themselves deeply for thirty days than for a longer period. For example, dropouts are heavy in eighteen week college courses.
- Thirty days divides nicely into four weeks. Most career people do their work and lifestyle planning on a week-by-week basis. This book is organized to take advantage of that excellent habit. After each week you will review your progress and set new goals for the next week.

The thirty-day system works. Give it a try!

YOU CAN DO IT!

CONTENTS

(continued next page)

CONTENTS (Continued)

TO THE READER

In thirty days you will be on your way to academic achievement—or you will have formed some bad habits that will prevent you from reaching your learning potential. This book, which you can read in less than one hour and then use as a guide for thirty days, can make the difference.

Please take time to thumb through the pages. This will give you an overview of what lies ahead. Then reread the introduction and preparation pages. After this, go week by week, so you will complete your first thirty college days and this program at the same time.

The College Experience will provide you with:

- Confidence to enroll in school and cope in the classroom
- A clear edge over others with similar goals
- Special tips on how to take advantage of student support services
- Techniques to deal with difficult professors
- Guidance on study habits: how to take exams, prepare oral and written reports, and participate in class.

Also included is a *College Major Preference Profile.* This exercise will help you start the process of selecting your college major.

As you accomplish these goals, keep in mind that professors, guidance experts, and other staff people are there to help you.

Good luck!

Elwood N. Chapman

THE INTERNATIONAL CAMPUS

A larger and more dynamic wave of people will return to college campuses between now and the turn of the century. Some will enter as full-time students. Far more will return for a single course or a part-time program to upgrade their careers. Some will return for higher degrees. Many older students will return to attend special seminars and noncredit classes, to increase their competencies and enhance their upward mobility. As our cultural mosaic changes (most campuses are becoming more international), the most popular course may be English as a Second Language. Age levels will range from eighteen to eighty. The average age on most campuses will be over thirty.

How do you fit into all of this?

The true purpose of all education is to help individuals reach their potential so they can make a significant contribution to the lives of others and society in general.

Your goal should be to reach your academic potential while building and enjoying relationships with others who are significantly different from you. To accomplish this, now may be the time to take a new look at yourself.

Getting Ready for Your First Day on Campus

> I'm a great believer in luck, and I find
> the harder I work the more of it I have.
> Thomas Jefferson

EXCESS BAGGAGE

College is a new beginning!

It is a journey into a different kind of world, like taking a cruise to a foreign land. Travel light and leave the following excess baggage behind:

- Job problems
- Home or family conflict
- Previous relationships that you may have outgrown
- Old stereotypes about learning, mental blocks, professors, career opportunities
- Bad habits such as chemical excesses, poor use of time, old ways of dealing with pressures
- Fears about taking tests, writing papers, speaking in class.

A college campus offers you four personal opportunities:

1. *A chance to build a new image.* Whatever you have been in the past is not important to the new people you will meet. Your professors, staff experts, and fellow students will give you the opportunity to build a "new you." In fact, they will help you do it.

2. *A chance to build more meaningful relationships.* For example, you will probably find new friends who have more in common with you than previous friends or co-workers. Relax and give them a chance to meet you.

3. *A chance to build a new confidence in yourself.* A side advantage to any form of education is the extra confidence it gives you to excel, both on campus and after you leave. Chances are good that in less than thirty days you will start feeling much better about yourself.

4. *A chance to discover new ways of learning.* However you have been learning in the past, you will find new ways to reach your creativity and mental capacity. Take advantage of each oppportunity!

Circle any of the above opportunities that apply to you.

WHY ARE YOU HERE?

The author, not satisfied with his own thoughts, recently interviewed students from all backgrounds on three college campuses. His basic question was: ''Why are you here?'' Some of the responses are listed below.

''I don't know what to do with my life yet. I need a solid career goal and I hope to find and prepare for it here.''

''For me it is just a matter of gaining more personal confidence. I tried the real world but I was not ready for it.''

''I've raised my family, so now I can seek my own fulfillment. It's fun to be here.''

''To qualify for a good entry job.''

''I need more ability to cope.''

''My company wanted me to get a degree. They are paying the tab. Why not?''

''It's knowledge I want—knowledge and decision-making skills.''

''My divorce settlement made getting a degree within reach.''

''I was falling behind in my computer skills.''

''I look at college as a rehearsal for the real drama that will take place later.''

''I'm not happy with myself at this stage of my life. I came back to college for a retread.''

''I need to get into the mainstream.''

''Society was bouncing me around, so I decided to come back and get a new attitude. Fortunately, there was some financial support I could take advantage of.''

''I think I'm an intellectual.''

''It's the only route to my career goal.''

''It will make me a more rounded person.''

''I'm tired of people getting promoted instead of me because they have degrees.''

BE TRUE TO YOUR FUTURE

Although it's never predictable, everyone has a future whether you're 20, 40, or 60. Guidance experts agree that the more one plans for the future, the better it will probably be. This is usually called life planning, and most colleges offer courses on the subject. Three basic steps are usually involved:

Step 1: Figure out the kind of future or lifestyle you desire.

Step 2: Find one or more careers that will take you to your future.

Step 3: Develop the skills and competencies in your chosen career so you can ride them to success.

COLLEGE IS THE BEST PLACE TO TAKE ALL THREE STEPS.

Step 1: Personal/academic counselors are there to help you design life goals. Either before or just after your first thirty days, stop by your own counseling center and get acquainted.

Step 2: Career specialists can introduce you to materials that will help you find a beginning or midlife career. These same people will keep you on the right track and see that you have the confidence to reach a good decision.

Step 3: Professors are there to help you learn the technical and other skills you need.

A college campus is where it all happens, and you can do it all while raising a family and holding down a full-time job. It doesn't matter where you are now; college is designed to help you be true to your future.*

---

*Elwood N. Chapman is the author of the highly acclaimed book *Be True to Your Future.* It is a practical guide that will help you identify your future, discover a career, find the right job, and stay current with the winds of change. You can order it using the form at the back of this book.

YOUR LEARNING ATTITUDE

On your first visit to a college campus, students of all ages and backgrounds seem to be scrambling in many directions without anything in common.

Not so!

Most students have a definite goal they want to reach. Some are full-time students headed for a degree. Some are part-time students, who may also be headed for a degree. Others seek to complete a single class successfully. Still others are on campus to reach other goals. All want upward mobility in their chosen careers or personal fulfillment of some kind.

Learning is what will get students to their goals. All entering students have what we might call a learning gap—a gap between the knowledge you have now and the knowledge you can have.

Everyone has a different potential. Yours may be extremely high or more modest. Regardless of where your potential is, there is a sizable gap between where you are now and where you can be. Your attitude toward learning is what will help you close your own personal gap.

On the following pages are two scales which you are encouraged to complete. One measures your general attitude towards college as a place to help you reach your potential. The other measures the confidence you have about academic achievement.

Both scales are designed to help you prepare for the thirty days ahead.

MEASURE YOUR ATTITUDE AND CONFIDENCE LEVEL ON THE NEXT TWO PAGES

ATTITUDE SCALE

How do you really feel about becoming a college student? Will you be proud of your new role? Competitive?

The following questions will help you assess your attitude toward college, so you can determine whether or not you should really be there. Answer the questions by a placing a check mark under *yes* or *no*.

	YES	NO
1. Do you wish to discover more about yourself?	☐	☐
2. Are you willing to do whatever it takes to survive in any course? Even to the point of accepting special help?	☐	☐
3. Do you really want to learn?	☐	☐
4. Do you see the connection between what you learn now and how it fits with your long-range future?	☐	☐
5. Can you become motivated about required subjects that you would prefer not to take?	☐	☐
6. Are you willing to reach out and benefit from intellectual conversations with others?	☐	☐
7. Can you have a positive attitude about adjusting to difficult professors, even if it means having a private conference?	☐	☐
8. If you run into academic trouble, will you see a counselor and accept suggestions?	☐	☐
9. Will you prepare for and attend every possible class, and participate when you get there?	☐	☐
10. If money becomes a problem, are you willing to work more hours or seek financial aid in order to stay with your program?	☐	☐

Total *yes* answers _____

If you had seven or more *yes* answers, you have a positive attitude toward college and your chances of surviving without a major setback are excellent. Have confidence in yourself, and strengthen it with good study habits. Also, make it an enjoyable and rewarding experience, not just a grind! If you have fewer than seven *yes* answers, you should ask yourself if you are ready for college at this time.

CONFIDENCE SCALE

You already have confidence in many areas. For example, you may feel fully competent in performing a certain job or driving an automobile. This scale is designed to help you evaluate your *academic confidence*—the confidence you currently possess about doing well in your class work. For each of these ten items, circle where you are *now* on a scale of 1 to 5.

I have all the academic self-confidence I need to become an honor student.	5 4 3 2 1	I have self-confidence in other areas—but academically I'm at the bottom.
Compared to others, I have an excellent vocabulary.	5 4 3 2 1	I lack self-confidence partly because of my weak vocabulary.
My ability to speak clearly, use the best grammer, and communicate well is tops.	5 4 3 2 1	I am so weak at verbal communication that I stay silent.
I am fully satisfied with my ability to listen, take notes, and learn in the classroom.	5 4 3 2 1	I'm at the bottom of the scale in classroom listening, note taking, and learning.
I find it easy to concentrate and study.	5 4 3 2 1	The moment I try to study I lose my concentration.
My basic survival skills—reading, writing, basic math—do not need improvement.	5 4 3 2 1	Improving my basic skills is absolutely necessary for me to gain academic confidence.
Getting more education is important to my career but not to my self-image.	5 4 3 2 1	The basic reason I am in college is to improve my self-image.
I always speak up in class and even challenge professors.	5 4 3 2 1	I do not have enough confidence to involve myself in classroom discussions.
I can communicate intelligently on any subject introduced socially.	5 4 3 2 1	I feel totally inadequate when it comes to social conversations.
Compared to my classmates, I deserve a 5 rating on my academic confidence.	5 4 3 2 1	Compared to my classmates, I am at the bottom in academic confidence.

Total Score _____

The lower you scored yourself on the scale, the more college can do for you if you make a strong effort.

DELAYED GRATIFICATION

College, as they say, can set you up for life! What you achieve academically now can upgrade your income, enhance your social and cultural experiences, and help you cope better with all future aspects of your life. Completing college (and the degree that goes with it) is delayed gratification (DG) on a master scale.

DG is the best available principle to follow if you wish to discipline yourself.

It works!
It's fun!
It's a great habit to form early!

Delayed gratification means to give yourself a reward but only *after you have reached a goal.* You set a short-term or long-term academic goal for yourself, determine the reward you will give yourself for reaching it, and psychologically hold the carrot (reward) in front of yourself until you achieve it. The principle can work on a daily, weekly, and monthly basis.

Daily DG: It is Tuesday and you have a tough class schedule, but you love cycling. You promise yourself a good ride providing you reach your maximum learning level in each class.

Weekly DG: You need to put in 20 hours of concentrated study next week, but there's a movie you want to see. If you reach your study goal you go; if not, you give yourself a less rewarding activity.

Monthly DG: You want to go on a three-day ski trip at the end of the term. You set a grade point average goal for yourself. If you reach it, the ski trip is on; if not, you cancel.

Obviously, the Delayed Gratification principle would apply to using this book. Write the reward you intend to give yourself after you have worked through this book successfully:

REWARD BOX

_____

_____

SUMMARY

The best thing about life on campus is that you can be yourself. A reentry student of 30 need not try to impress a freshman ten years younger. Or vice versa. Everyone can relax and be themselves. It is under these conditions that the best kind of learning takes place. Read the statements below and check ☑ the ones you agree with. Total agreement is not expected.

☐ EVERYONE GETS A FRESH START. Whatever your past history may be, your professors, advisors, and classmates will consider you are starting from scratch. Great feeling!

☐ ANXIETY IS NORMAL AT THE BEGINNING. Most new students have apprehensions. What demands will professors put on me? Will I embarrass myself in class? Do I have the confidence to face these new academic challenges? Like a new job in a strange city, college life entails some adjustments. You will feel more competent after the first week.

☐ I NEED TO LEARN THE ROPES. Each professor has his or her own rules. Observation is the first priority; classroom participation will come later. Sometimes it is best to get some inside help from a classmate who has had previous experience with the instructor.

☐ I WANT TO MAKE NEW FRIENDS. Without making a few new friends you will be missing out on some of the value of your college experience. Do not hesitate to reach out both academically and socially.

☐ DELAYED GRATIFICATION IS MY KIND OF STRATEGY. I believe in setting daily, weekly, and monthly goals and giving myself suitable rewards when such goals are reached. This is how I intend to operate at college.

☐ EVERYONE CAN ESTABLISH HIS OR HER OWN STYLE. You can have as much or as little contact with people as you like. You can dress to suit yourself. You can strive for A grades or be satisfied with less. You can become deeply involved in upgrading your competencies and other intellectual pursuits or you can adopt a ''get by'' attitude.

It is important that you enjoy your college experience and find your own ''comfort zone'' both in and out of the classroom. But your commitment is to learning. Your style should not neglect your real reason for being on campus.

CASE PROBLEMS

The College Experience provides more than twenty short case problems. When the book is used in orientation classes or small seminar groups, the case problems are excellent for discussion. They can also be beneficial on an individual, self-help basis. When using the book alone, the reader is encouraged to read each case, write out a decision, and then turn to the back of the book and compare his or her answer with the suggestions of the author. These will be found starting on page 76.

Case 1. Rod is back in college at age 29. He has just returned from a session in which his advisor suggested he take a special six-hour orientation and how-to-study course. The program is offered on a voluntary, noncredit basis for all beginning students.

"I've decided to skip that orientation class they recommend," Rod said to his friend Mitch over a cup of coffee. "It might pay off for those who are younger, but at my age it would be a waste of time. After all, I've had five years of business experience. I have my career all picked out, and I'm highly motivated to achieve. Besides. If the course were really worthwhile, they would make it mandatory and give us credit."

Is Rod making the right decision? _____

_____

_____

Case 2. Joyce, a reentry student, feels lost, uncomfortable, and inadequate after a difficult divorce. Her self-image is poor. She does not have the self-confidence to make new friends. To remedy the situation, she has decided to impress her classmates and earn their friendship through intellectual achievements. She will spend more time preparing for her courses than other students do.

Is her solution a good one? _____

_____

_____

Case 3. Jim, a very bright young man, received straight A grades in all the difficult mathematics courses in high school. He could have had his choice of colleges, but he was not interested because he had formed a very successful rock group. The group cut several records and enjoyed some top-flight bookings. Jim has also had some success as a songwriter. Despite this success, he is uneasy about his future. Will he eventually tire of the show-business environment? Will his group be able to survive over the long run? Recently Jim has had a few thoughts about enrolling in college as a full-time student.

Should he do so? _____

_____

Getting Your Study Habits in Order

> Do what you can, with what you have, where you are.
>
> Theodore Roosevelt

THE FIRST DAY

Some people, even after thirty years have elapsed, remember many details of their first day on campus. Why is this?

The primary reason is fear over whether you will be accepted. The stakes are extremely high. You want to prove to yourself and others that you can handle things. You want to prove to your peers that you can learn and compete. Your ego is deeply involved. No wonder new students get nervous their first day on campus!

To compound the problem, the first days on any campus can be frustrating. Parking problems occur. Registration and other lines can be long. Most new students get lost a few times. Then there is the problem of classes that are closed or cancelled. Sometimes all one can do is find a quiet bench somewhere and view the entire process from a distance, hoping that everything will fall into place on day two.

Regardless of what happens, hang on to your positive attitude and follow these tips:

- Admit you are frustrated and nervous and talk to other students about it. You might find someone to go through the experience with you.
- Don't wait for others to be nice or talk to you. Extend your own hand of friendship first.
- Laugh frustrations away. Above all, do not allow the experience to turn you against the college.

Your first day is critical to your future on campus. You can't afford to let anything turn you negative and slow your adjustment. It's up to you to *make* your first day a success, regardless of the difficulties you face.

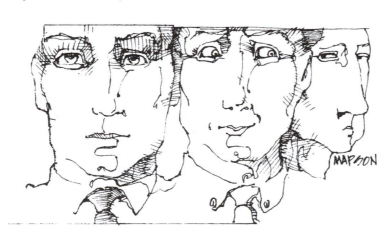

YOU CAN'T LEARN UNLESS YOU LISTEN!

Effective listening is the key to success on any campus and in any lecture hall or seminar. Good listening is especially important the first week. You will be receiving reading assignments and learning about grading procedures. You will be getting instructions about how to use the campus library, the laboratory, and so on. You may have been able to get away with daydreaming in high school or at work, but you will pay a much higher price for failure on campus. Unlike high school teachers, college instructors won't hold your hand.

How do you rate your listening ability?

OUTSTANDING	EXCELLENT	GOOD	POOR	WEAK

Are you satisfied? How can you improve your listening skills for the critical days ahead? Answer the statements below and see how.

	YES	NO
1. I will listen to what is being said rather than evaluate who is saying it.	☐	☐
2. I will listen with my eyes as well as my ears.	☐	☐
3. I will refrain from interrupting until I am sure I have received the message correctly.	☐	☐
4. If I am not sure about the message, I will raise my hand and ask for clarification.	☐	☐
5. I will take good notes but not become so involved that I miss what else the professor is saying.	☐	☐
6. I will make sure I am in the best physical position to hear the message.	☐	☐
7. I will keep my nervousness under control by keeping everything in perspective.	☐	☐
8. I will concentrate and not fake my attention.	☐	☐
9. I *want* to hear every message.	☐	☐
10. I will be a patient listener.		

If you gave yourself seven or more *yes* answers, you appear to be ready for your listening responsibilities in college. If you gave yourself fewer than seven *yes* answers, some attitude adjustment on your part may be necessary.*

The Business of Listening by Diane Bone may be ordered using the form in the back of this book.

TWO SUGGESTIONS

Your preliminary preparation for your campus learning experience is complete. At this point you have probably either read or taken a casual look at all of the pages in this book. How should you use the material on a week-by-week basis?

Two suggestions:

1. Read and study all the first Week One pages once more before you attend your first class.

2. Refer to the relevant pages DURING the first week as you settle into your study habits.

Whatever the procedure you work out the first week, stay with it for the following three weeks—making improvements as you go.

At the end of each week you will be invited to complete a personal assessment of your progress and to set some new goals for the following week. Give this your best shot and you will be pleased with the results. Keep in mind, the sooner you get on a winning academic path the more pleasurable and fulfilling college will be!

HOW TO TAKE LECTURE NOTES

Are you a good note taker? Do you follow the proven guidelines? If not, the following tips should help you save time, get rid of some confusion, and improve your grades:

TIP 1. *Use a single, large, loose-leaf binder.* This permits you to add or discard sheets of paper as needed. By using tabular dividers, you have a section for each course you are taking. Make this binder your constant companion during class and study hours. Always begin your notes for each lecture or each chapter on a separate page, assigning the page a title and a date.

TIP 2. *Apply the Record-and-Condense method.* Take notes during a class period and then condense them into clear and concise thoughts before the day is over. Note taking does not mean recording every word the professor says, or copying each word of a chapter you read. It means writing down the key ideas in an orderly manner that makes sense to you and that will be easy to recall later. Use your own outline form. Include concepts, facts, quotations, special vocabulary, and related ideas that will help you understand the topic covered. Extract what you need but don't overdo the detail. Record this material on the left side of the page, leaving about a three-inch margin free on the right.

TIP 3. *Use the Review-and-Revise method.* When reading your textbook, underline or highlight those passages you want to remember. Later, when you review, write in the page margin your own interpretation of the idea so you will be able to remember it and express it in your own words. To summarize the notes you have taken in class, write your interpretation in the three-inch margin of your notes.

TIP 4. *Reflect on each topic before undertaking the next one.* Reflecting is necessary if you are to retain what you have learned. It takes only a few minutes and can frequently be done in class while waiting for the professor to begin speaking. This step also provides continuity to the course.

SHOULD YOU TAKE A HOW-TO-STUDY COURSE?

Obviously, anyone can profit from taking a good course on how to study. This scale is designed to tell you how *badly* you might need such a course. It should be taken your first week on campus, preferably the same day you purchase your textbooks. Read the statements on both ends of the scale and then circle where you feel you fall. A 5 indicates no help is needed. A 1 signals all possible help is required.

I can study for long periods without becoming depressed.	5 4 3 2 1	I almost always become depressed when I study.
I already know the basic study techniques.	5 4 3 2 1	I do not know any how-to-study techniqes.
I know exactly how to prepare notes for review purposes.	5 4 3 2 1	I need help on how to take notes when I study.
I have no trouble organizing material into study units.	5 4 3 2 1	I need help because I cannot organize my study material.
My concentration time-span is fully adequate for my needs.	5 4 3 2 1	My concentration time-span is far too short.
I know exactly what to cover in a chapter; I skip only unimportant material.	5 4 3 2 1	I find myself skipping material I know is important.
I'm motivated to study because I know how to do it.	5 4 3 2 1	I'm not motivated to study; in fact, I get frustrated when I try.
I feel I can learn twice as much as most students in less time.	5 4 3 2 1	I take twice as long to learn half as much as I should.
I have a positive attitude toward studying.	5 4 3 2 1	I have a negative attitude toward studying.
I'm an outstanding reader.	5 4 3 2 1	I'm an extremely weak reader.

Total Score _____

If you scored 35 or higher on the scale, chances are you know how to study. If you scored under 35, a how-to-study course would greatly enhance your study techniques, save you time in the long run, and help you get better grades.

THREE STUDY THEORIES

1. The Put-in-Your-Time Theory

The naive approach that students use in preparing for examinations could be described as the Put-in-Your-Time theory. The basic idea here is that if you schedule enough time to study for each class and then actually devote this time to preparation, you will achieve your academic goals. This is a naive approach because there is little correlation between the time a student devotes to learning and how much he or she actually learns. A fast reader with good comprehension learns just as much as a slow reader with good comprehension. To be sure, adequate time is necessary, but the student with good concentration using the right techniques can easily learn twice as much in half the time as the student who simply puts in time.

2. The Press-Stress Theory

Some students wait until the last minute to prepare for an exam because the time limitation automatically presses them into greater concentration. Usually this is not a good idea. The theory, however, can take a more positive form. For example, you can press yourself into a temporary and harmless stress situation without waiting until the last minute. Suppose you have allocated four hours on your weekly study schedule to prepare for your chemistry class, but you want to participate in an activity that requires extra time. To accommodate both, you might press yourself into learning in two hours what you normally would have taken four hours to learn. In short, you deliberately press yourself into a stressful time frame so you will learn faster. This method is recommended only for the experienced student who has learned many solid study techniques and knows how to make it work.

3. The Prepare-Review-Relax Theory

This theory encompasses most of the traditional principles of reliable study patterns:

1. Prepare at your best pace ahead of time.
2. Review what you have learned the day or night before you take an examination.
3. Spend a little time relaxing so you can get a good night's sleep and be mentally alert when you take the examination.

This theory is the direct opposite of the Press-Stress theory. It encourages the student to use the right techniques and avoid stress. For most students, this theory makes sense. It is especially recommended for the beginning student.

> The theory I intend to put into practice is:
>   The Put-in-Your-Time theory   ☐
>   The Press-Stress theory   ☐
>   The Prepare-Review-Relax theory   ☐

STUDY ATTITUDES

The question most frequently asked by beginning college students of all ages is: "How can I learn to study more effectively?" Concentration is a habit many have never developed. Learning in class through group discussion is easy. Isolating oneself and digging out information on your own is more difficult.

The inability to concentrate and learn from cold printed material is not unusual. College students are not the only ones plagued with the problem. Business executives, successful writers, and even professors have this problem, too. So don't worry about being the only one facing this challenge—you have plenty of company both on and off campus.

To learn to study effectively, you need to develop the right attitude toward study, become acquainted with a few study theories, and learn to use proven, well-defined study techniques.

How? Here are three suggestions:

SHARPEN YOUR CURIOSITY! First, build an attitude of curiosity. Look at each chapter or assignment as a new world to conquer. You must want to read not because it's required but because you are curious. What is the author really trying to say? Why does the reader need this information? What can you learn that's new?

BECOME A CRITICAL READER! Second, challenge what the author says. Be critical. Why did your professor select this book? Why does it take the author so long to say so little? What's important? What's trivial? What's worth remembering? What isn't? When you open a book, take a critical view. Challenge the author every page of the way.

BECOME A COMPETITIVE STUDENT! Third, be competitive. Try to be informed so you can outthink your classmates and, if possible, your professor. To play the education game, you need private study as ammunition. Without individual study and learning, you can't compete in class, on tests, or in written reports. You'll be an observer instead of a participant.

STUDY TECHNIQUES

Once you have developed a positive study attitude and selected the study theory that you believe will be most effective for you, study techniques pay off. Here are some tips to consider. Keep in mind that you will eventually develop your own, individual study style that helps you achieve your academic goals with the least expenditure of time.

STUDY WHERE THE ACTION ISN'T. Individual study is a lonely business. It takes a strong person to shut out the rest of the world and sweat it out alone. But you *must* do it to create an atmosphere that will permit you to concentrate. A comfortable place, the right lighting, and right tools (dictionary, pencils, slide rule, paper, books) are all essential.

SHIFT YOUR MIND QUICKLY INTO A STUDY GEAR. Sit down at your study station, get your notebook and pencil ready, open your textbook, and then say to yourself, "Whatever this author has to tell me in this chapter, I'm going to learn—and fast."

ONCE YOUR MIND IS IN GEAR, KEEP IT THERE. If you are not careful, you'll lose your forward motion. This can happen if you read so fast you miss the meaning of the words.

KNOW YOUR STUDY LIMITATIONS. You will reach a point of diminishing returns in any prolonged study period. Your eyes will tire. Your body will become tense. Your mind will start to spin away from the subject material. Don't force yourself too far beyond your natural study limits.

REWARD YOURSELF. Most students can concentrate better and study harder if they have set up an immediate reward. Give yourself something pleasant to do *after* you have done some profitable studying—not before.

READ A GOOD HOW-TO-STUDY BOOK OR TAKE A STUDY SKILLS COURSE. The techniques presented in this section can help you significantly in solving your study problems, but you may need more extensive help. Several excellent books have been written on the subject.*

---

*An outstanding book is *Study Skills Strategies* by Uelaine Langefeld. You can order it using the form at the back of this book.

MORE STUDY TECHNIQUES

USE THE RULE-OF-THREE TREATMENT. In reading a chapter, try following these three steps:

1. Take a few minutes to look over the titles and subtitles to get a general idea of what it is about. Scan. What do you think the author is trying to say? Build up your curiosity so the chapter will be more interesting.

2. Go back over it paragraph by paragraph, giving it the colored-pencil treatment. Underline or highlight the important titles and sentences—the messages that hit you as important, significant, or worth remembering. Search for and underline the significant and forget the trival.

3. Sit back and rethink the chapter for a few minutes. Take it apart in your mind. Try to comprehend the overall message. Then in your notebook write out the important ideas as you see them. Also reference key page numbers in the text.

READ IT—TALK IT—REVIEW IT. Talk to yourself as you follow the rule-of-three approach explained above. Sound ridiculous? Far from it. Research shows that you learn more if you verbalize, recite, or talk to yourself as you go through the material. If you find a section that is especially difficult, follow this routine:

1. Read it, talking to yourself as you go.

2. After you have finished, tell yourself what it said that you should remember.

3. If you can't remember very much, tackle the section again before going on.

Time-consuming and clumsy? Perhaps. But if you can't get the message another way, why not give it a try?

Read it—talk it—review it. It works.

SORT OUT KEY FACTS AND FIGURES FOR SPECIAL ATTENTION. Few students have a photographic memory, so you'll need to make a game of it to succeed in remembering special facts and figures. A good technique is to make a written list of key facts as you go through a chapter. Putting them on 3″ × 5″ cards is also effective—you can thumb through them in a few seconds. Once you have accumulated your list, concentrate on it for a few moments. The psychology is simple. In addition to reading and verbalizing the facts and figures, you have written them out in your own handwriting. Repetition is an excellent learning device. Cards are also easy to carry around for quick reference before classes.

TIME MANAGEMENT

College students quickly discover that time is elusive and tricky. It is the easiest thing in the world to lose and the most difficult to control. At first, as you look toward the end of the term, it may appear that you have more time than you need. Yet time has a way of slipping through your fingers like sand. You may suddenly find there is no way to stretch the little time left to cover all your academic obligations. When this happens, many students panic. The answer? Early control.

Time is dangerous. If you don't control it, it will control you. While you are a college student, time management will probably be your greatest problem.

Skeptical? Here are comments from a few students who ignored the problems:

> "At the beginning I squandered time as though I had an unlimited supply. I had poor study habits, daydreamed a great deal, and got mixed up in stupid involvements. Then everything hit me at once. If I hadn't received the time management message when I did, my college career would have been finished."
>
> "I thought that time management would come automatically—that the system itself would line me up. It was almost a fatal mistake. It took me six weeks to realize that time control was 100 percent my baby. If I didn't control it, time would disappear."

All college students need some "therapeutic" fun and relaxation to dissipate pressures. But be sure that you are not squandering large blocks of time. If this happens, you will eventually find yourself in trouble in your courses and discover that your free time is no longer enjoyable.

"SORRY, JOE. IT'S STUDY TIME TONIGHT."

TIME SCHEDULING TIPS

PREPARE A WEEKLY STUDY SCHEDULE. Use the model schedule and the schedule form on the following pages to prepare your schedule. Additional copies can be made for a three-ring binder so your schedule is always available.

BE REALISTIC. When you plan time for important compositions, special tests, and projects, schedule enough time to do a high-quality job. If you underestimate the time necessary, it may force you to discard your normal pattern and devote night and day to crash efforts.

MAKE YOUR STUDY TIME SUIT THE COURSE. Some experts say you should schedule three hours of study for every hour in class; others say two hours of preparation per class hour should be sufficient. How much study time you schedule for each course hour depends on four factors: (1) your ability, (2) the difficulty of the class, (3) the grade you hope to achieve, and (4) how well you use your study time. But regardless of the variables, you should schedule not less than one hour to study for each classroom hour. In many cases, more study time will be required.

KEEP YOUR SCHEDULE FLEXIBLE. It is vital to replan your schedule every week to ensure a degree of flexibility as you move through the term. For example, as you approach midterms or final exams, you will want to juggle your schedule to provide more time for reviewing. When a research project is assigned, you will want to provide an additional block of time sufficient to do a good job. Try to schedule such important tasks at your most effective peak during the day. You will do a better job in less time than you would need during a less effective period. Experiment to find out what your effectiveness rhythm is and then use it to your advantage.

USE THE 20-20-20 FORMULA. For students who work about twenty hours each week and take a full college load, the 20-20-20 formula makes sense. This means you will be in classes approximately 20 hours each week, work 20 hours, and study a minimum of 20 hours. This formula was used to prepare Barry's schedule, which appears on the next page.

STUDY EACH CLASS DAY. Some concentrated study each day is better than many study hours one day and none the next. As you work out your individual schedule, try to include a minimum of two study hours each day. This will not only keep the study habit alive but will keep you up-to-date on your class assignments and projects.

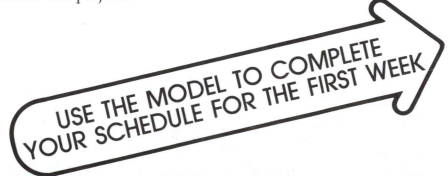

USE THE MODEL TO COMPLETE YOUR SCHEDULE FOR THE FIRST WEEK

MODEL SCHEDULE

Analyze Barry's study schedule, then use it as a model to construct your own schedule on the next page.

	BARRY'S SCHEDULE **Oct. 10-16**						
	Monday	**Tuesday**	**Wednesday**	**Thursday**	**Friday**	**Saturday**	**Sunday**
8:00	MATH	MATH	MATH	STUDY HIST	MATH	WORK	SLEEP
9:00	STUDY CHEM	HIST	STUDY CHEM	HIST	STUDY CHEM		SLEEP
10:00	CHEM	HIST	CHEM	HIST	CHEM		CHORES
11:00	FREE	PE SWIM	FREE	PE SWIM	CHEM		CHORES
12:00	LUNCH	LUNCH	LUNCH	LUNCH	LUNCH		
1:00	ENG	ENG	ENG	CHEM LAB	ENG		STUDY
2:00	STUDY MATH LIBRARY	STUDY MATH LIBRARY	STUDY LIBRARY		STUDY MATH LIBRARY		
3:00	FREE	CHORES	FREE		WORK		
4:00	DINNER	CHORES	DINNER		WORK		
5:00	WORK	DINNER	WORK	DINNER	DINNER		
6:00		STUDY HIST		STUDY ENG.	FREE	FREE	FREE
7:00		STUDY		STUDY ENG.			FREE
8:00		HIST		STUDY ENG.			STUDY
9:00		STUDY HIST		STUDY			STUDY
10:00		FREE					FREE

YOUR WEEKLY STUDY SCHEDULE

Use the form below to make a schedule for your first week at college.

Please follow these steps:
1. Record your class and lab periods.
2. Add your work hours, if any.
3. Fill in the study hours you feel are necessary.

Week of _____	Monday	Tuesday	Wednesday	Thursday	Friday	Saturday	Sunday
8:00							
9:00							
10:00							
11:00							
12:00							
1:00							
2:00							
3:00							
4:00							
5:00							
6:00							
7:00							
8:00							
9:00							
10:00							

CASE PROBLEMS

Read each case and write out your answer. Then turn to pages 76-77 to see the author's suggested answers.

Case 4. Linda wants to improve her self-image by losing weight. She also wants to fly home for Christmas knowing that all of her academic work is up to the highest possible level. She makes a contract with herself to lose twelve pounds and study four additional hours per week between now and her departure date.

What are her chances of success? _____

_____

_____

Case 5. Toby is a college freshman. He is in an Upward Bound program designed to help minority students adjust and survive. Since he has a weak background in English, is a slow reader, and hasn't yet developed sound study habits, Toby's advisor has suggested that he take only makeup courses the first term.

Do you agree? _____

_____

_____

Case 6. Martha has decided to major in history. She considers herself a good reader but knows that some other students have better reading speed and comprehension. Last week her advisor suggested she might consider taking a special reading course to increase her speed and comprehension. Martha discovered that if she takes the course, she'll have to postpone a course she really wants to take. She then decided to go to the library and find a book that would help improve her reading skills, thinking she could accomplish the same results on a do-it-yourself basis.

*Do you agree?*_____

_____

_____

Case 7. Yesterday Jack heard about the campus financial aid center and how much money was available for grants. He is taking a full academic program and is under financial pressure. But he feels that because he comes from a middle-income family, he would not be eligible.

Should he investigate? _____

_____

_____

FIRST WEEK ASSESSMENT

This exercise is a personal progress report. It is designed to help you pinpoint areas of success or areas where renewed emphasis is needed. Complete this assessment only after you have been in a class or classes for a full week. Check ☑ the appropriate box. Be totally honest with yourself.

	FULLY SATISFIED	PARTIALLY SATISFIED	NOT SATISFIED
Did I take advantage of my classroom learning opportunities?	☐	☐	☐
How do I feel about my study station? Is it the best available?	☐	☐	☐
What about my level of concentration in the classroom?	☐	☐	☐
What about my level of concentration when I am reading?	☐	☐	☐
Am I speaking up enough in the classroom?	☐	☐	☐
What about my note-taking procedure?	☐	☐	☐
Am I studying at the right time?	☐	☐	☐
How do I feel about my motivation to learn?	☐	☐	☐
What about making new friends?	☐	☐	☐
Are my listening skills all they should be?	☐	☐	☐

Based on my answers and other experiences, I intend to concentrate on improving the following areas next week:

1. _____
2. _____
3. _____
4. _____
5. _____

Moving Ahead
with Confidence

Always take a job that is too big for you.
Harry Emerson Foskick

STOP PROCRASTINATING

Why are college students so good at procrastinating? Listed below are ten possible reasons. Check ☑ the three that are most applicable to you.

☐ Laziness   ☐ Lack of priorities
☐ Fear of failure   ☐ Depression
☐ Boredom   ☐ Physical fatigue
☐ Outside distractions   ☐ Lack of analytical ability
☐ Dependence on others   ☐ Physical disability

Dr. James R. Sherman in his book *Stop Procrastinating** delivers eighteen proven techniques that will help any college student. Here are a few:

1. ***SUBDIVIDE INTO SMALLER PARTS.*** Reach your academic goal class by class, day by day, week by week.

2. ***SET GOALS.*** Without goals you are ''hanging out'' on campus. You are not a student.

3. ***ANALYZE REASONS.*** Go back to the list of reasons for procrastinating and make a commitment.

4. ***TACKLE YOUR TOUGHEST COURSE FIRST.*** If you conquer your most difficult course, your fears will not spread to others.

5. ***VISUALIZE COMPLETION AND SUCCESS.*** Picture in your mind the great feeling you will have upon reaching your academic goals. Picture the rewards you will have earned and will be able to give yourself.

---

* You can order Dr. Sherman's book using the order form at the back of this book.

FALL IN LOVE
WITH YOUR TEXTS

This may sound like overkill, but the attitude you develop towards your textbooks determines, to some extent, what you learn from them. Please consider these points:

1. You victimize yourself when you become negative toward a text and, as a result, read it grudgingly. Your mind is not fully open. You forget good reading techniques. Instead of what could be a rewarding learning experience, the effort is a waste of time.

2. A textbook is designed to present research, principles, theories, ideas—it is not designed to entertain you. Much of the material you must dig out and evaluate on your own. This is part of the learning process and being a college student. Why fight it?

3. You read a textbook differently from novels, music magazines, or other publications designed to be pleasurable. You can't expect to transfer the positive attitude you may have about reading *Rolling Stone* to a chemistry text.

HOW TO READ A TEXT →

LEARN TO READ EFFICIENTLY

Joyce Turley, in *Speed-Reading in Business**, provides the tools necessary to improve your reading speed, retention, and comprehension. Here are three easy-to-apply suggestions from her book:

1. Use the multiple reading technique.

   - Preview the book or article first. Inspect everything, including the index, introduction, cover, and date of publication.
   - Do an overview. Quickly look through the book so you can program your brain on how to use it.
   - Read for comprehension.
   - Review what you have read after reading it.
   - Create an instant replay so you go over key points.

2. Use your finger as a pacer.

   - A pacer is any object to help you follow what you are reading. Our eyes tend to jerk but we can move them smoothly (without moving our heads) when we use a pacer. Your index finger is the most convenient pacer to use. Or you may prefer to use a bookmark or highlighter pen.

3. Learn to read faster.

   - Push your brain and your pacer
   - Refuse to linger over difficult words (look them up later).
   - Don't use your lips as you read.
   - Block out all noise.

Naturally, you will find a reading improvement program on your campus. If you are a poor reader, enroll in this course. You may read up to one thousand hours during your college years. Why not reduce it to six hundred or fewer, with greater retention?

---

* *Speed Reading in Business,* published by Crisp Publications, can be ordered using the form at the back of this book.

DO A COURSE ANALYSIS

The first week or honeymoon is over, and you are getting acquainted with the academic challenges you face. It is time to design a winning strategy for each course. To accomplish this, it is necessary to view each class as a separate challenge, a unique experience, a game with different rules. An architect designs a new set of blueprints for each structure. A pilot needs a special flight plan for each departure. A coach needs an individual game for each contest.

Why do you need a separate plan for each course?

The answer is fundamental. Each subject has its own peculiar characteristics. Each instructor treats his subject uniquely. You need a special plan for each course because the strategy that works for one may not be effective for another. Furthermore, different courses have differing importance to your career and personal goals.

By planning ahead, you can avoid the crisis that causes students to drop some courses in order to survive in the others. If you follow the suggestions in this section, you should be able to devise a simple, successful plan to reach your goal for each course without wasting your energies. College courses seem to fall generally into three categories:

- The constant-discipline course
- The delayed-action course
- The self-involving course

Decide which category each of your courses fits into. Then use the following suggestions to develop your plan for each course.

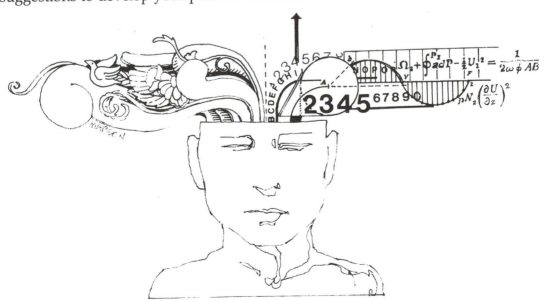

CONSTANT-DISCIPLINE COURSES

The constant-discipline courses usually require daily outside study or even written assignments for each hour spent in the classroom. In such classes pressure is applied constantly. Mathematics, foreign language, English composition, shorthand, accounting, and many science classes fall into this category. In handling these courses keep in mind that the subject matter is usually taught in sequence. You must learn today's lesson in order to understand tomorrow's. Some educators refer to these as *block* disciplines because one block of learning is built upon another. In other words, if you don't fully understand the first blocks of learning, you may not be able to understand future blocks—and the whole course may fall down upon you.

What should be your strategy in taking a constant-discipline course? Check ☑ any item below that you pledge to incorporate into your strategy:

☐ 1. *Determine to stay in control from the very beginning.* Allocate more study time than you expect to use. Don't miss a class or an assignment.

☐ 2. *Get your homework done as soon as possible after each class session.* You will do a better job in less time if you complete assignments when the material is still fresh in your mind.

☐ 3. *Don't become complacent and lose control.* Be alert in the classroom. Try to stay ahead of both the professor and your classmates.

☐ 4. *Anticipate potential problems before they occur.* If you are making mistakes in your homework without knowing why, see your instructor in a hurry. Usually only a small margin of error is allowed.

☐ 5. *Keep your eyes open about your own progress.* Gauge your classroom attention and learning speed with others. Compare your study concentration span with acceptable standards. Stick to your assignment schedule.

☐ 6. *Constantly evaluate your progress on tests and written assignments.* If you are not doing well, see your professor immediately to find out why. If you need tutoring, get it.

Constant-discipline courses are demanding. Students may be tempted to choose less demanding college majors, leading to less satisfying careers. If your goal requires that you successfully complete one or more discipline courses, stick with them even if you must curtail some other activities. The long-term reward will justify the sacrifice.

DELAYED-ACTION COURSES

In delayed-action courses you attend lectures, do outside reading, and take relatively few tests. In some cases, your final grade depends on your performance in only two or three examinations, which are usually delayed until you have forgotten much of what you have learned. You don't have the opportunity to benefit from several small tests beforehand. You don't have the security of earning a grade by turning in a weekly assignment. Literature courses, many business courses (such as marketing, salesmanship, and business law), and most social science courses (such as history, economics, sociology, and psychology) traditionally fall into this category.

These are obviously dangerous courses for several reasons:

1. It is too easy to postpone or delay outside reading until the big test is close at hand.

2. By the time the first test is given and you discover how well you are doing, the term may be half over.

3. The discipline is left entirely up to you. You must organize the information in a logical manner as you accumulate it so that when a major test finally comes, you have good recall.

What is your best strategy in preparing a plan for delayed-action courses? Check ☑ any that you plan to use:

☐ 1. *Discipline yourself to take good lecture notes.* Revise your notes later, so they will be well organized for reviewing before a big exam.

☐ 2. *Do your outside reading regularly.* As you do it, take notes or follow an underlining technique that works for you. Casual reading may leave you unprepared when test day arrives.

☐ 3. *Read everything about the subject that time will permit.* Adopt a serious learning attitude toward the subject.

☐ 4. *Involve yourself in classroom discussions.* You'll find that what you hear in class and what you read outside will have more meaning. Professors are supposed to make their subject exciting to their students. If your instructor fails in this respect, do it on your own.

☐ 5. *When you get your first test back, go over it carefully.* Study your mistakes so you won't repeat them later. Analyze what type of examination it was so you can adjust your study strategy and improve your performance the next time around.

Once you have planned your strategy, check it out with your instructor. He or she may have some helpful suggestions. Make no mistake, delayed-action courses spell trouble for many students. Do not underestimate them. Without a sound, well-executed plan, you may have to bail out.

SELF-INVOLVING COURSES

Not all courses fit into the first two classifications. Some have peculiar differences that require separate analysis on your part. For example, creative arts classes (art, music, drama, public speaking) make special demands on students. Other courses—such as science, drafting, electronics, nursing, and merchandising—require laboratory work. Such courses often have different learning climates, odd schedules, unusual standards, and special demands. These differences are chiefly the result of the special nature of the course content and the treatment the professor wishes to give it. Most instructors anticipate that students will eventually involve themselves in the course without any outside pressure. There are few examinations, if any. At times there is a minimum of supervision. Self-learning, permissive schedules, individual progress charts, and similar techniques characterize these highly diverse courses.

How do you make a plan for such courses? Here are three suggestions:

1. *Learn first-hand what is expected and what is involved.* Make an appointment with the professor and ask him or her about the course. This step is especially important if the course is outside your special field of interest.

2. *Check your interest level.* Courses in this classification are high-interest classes for many students. If the course is your favorite, guard against getting over-involved; if you find you have a low interest, force yourself to become more involved in order to survive.

3. *Get involved.* Many self-involving courses are especially difficult for timid students who feel they are not welcome in the group and consequently stay on the sidelines. If you can force yourself to become involved, the course can be a welcome relief from your more disciplined classes. It can give necessary balance to your total program. Most advisors suggest that every student should have at least one high-interest or personally involving course each term.

What are the dangers in taking such courses?

1. You may deemphasize the course.
2. You may have to compensate for less talent.
3. You may not be able to handle the freedom.

PUTTING IT ALL TOGETHER

To summarize, review, and apply what you have learned for your second week, write the course(s) you are taking under the proper category below:

Delayed-Action Courses	Constant-Discipline Courses	Self-Involvement Courses
_____	_____	_____
_____	_____	_____
_____	_____	_____
_____	_____	_____
_____	_____	_____
_____	_____	_____

After you have devised a separate plan for each course, you still face the most difficult problem: *You must balance your courses so that you don't favor one or two and neglect the others.* You may want to achieve an exceptionally high grade in one course but certainly not at the expense of a very poor grade in another. For example, if you spend all your study time on constant-discipline courses, your delayed-action and self-involving courses may suffer. If you become overcommitted to a self-involving course, your work in others may take a tailspin. Balance is essential if you are to complete several courses successfully at the same time.

Many students fall behind and drop courses because (1) they fail to do enough analysis and planning for each course at the beginning of the term, and (2) they fail to monitor their progress in each course. Sometimes it is necessary to drop one course in order to survive in others. Obviously, it is better to drop one course and complete the others successfully than to drop out of school altogether. It should be your goal, however, to survive in every course you take.

CASE PROBLEMS

Read each case and write out your answer. Then compare your answers with the author's suggestions on page 77.

Case 8. Tony has a hard time staying awake in Mr. Bush's history lectures. Although Mr. Bush obviously knows what he is talking about, he is more a historian than a teacher. Much of the time he reads from his notes or the text and seldom permits questions. Yesterday, Tony inadvertently discovered that Professor Bush does not record or require attendance and that many students pass his examinations by simply reading on their own. Tony decided to try this approach. Instead of going to class, he would read in the library. Another student promised to tell him in advance about any special assignments or examinations that come up.

Is Tony making a smart move? _____

_____

_____

Case 9. Judy is a chemistry major. She is doing fine so far in all of her courses, but she feels it won't last long. She must work more than thirty hours per week to survive, and she is beginning to feel pressure. She comes from a rather high-income family, but her parents are separated and she refuses to accept their help.

Should she investigate a government interest-free loan?

_____

_____

Case 10. Terri is confused and frustrated about her future. Everything she attempts academically seems to lead nowhere. She figures the best thing in her life right now is Hal, who wants to marry her as soon as possible. Terri is tempted to say *yes* because Hal is very kind and sensitive to her needs. He has told her that if she works now to help him complete college, he will return the favor later. Terri's parents seem to like Hal.

Should she marry him? _____

_____

_____

Case 11. Mario, at 29, feels he is more handicapped than other returning students his age. He grew up in a family that spoke only Spanish. Although he is bilingual, his English is weak. He raised himself to a supervisory position in the factory where he works, but he does not consider this background any help to him. He dropped out of high school fourteen years ago and is fearful of the classroom, where he might be embarrassed. His long-term goal is to get into upper management. He must have a degree to do this.

Is Mario's goal impossible to reach? _____

_____

_____

BALANCE

Looking back on your first week should provide some guidelines for adjustments to your weekly study schedule for next week.

How did you balance any home responsibilities, job involvements, and leisure hours with your study hours?

- Are you working too many hours?
- Are you neglecting your exercise program?
- Are you spending too much time taking care of home problems?
- Is your academic program receiving top priority?

Please review the schedule you prepared for your first week. Make a new schedule for your second week, using the form on the next page. In doing this, try a better balance on all the time-consuming factors in your life. Once you decide how many hours you can spend studying, divide these hours among your various courses. Use the analysis you made in the Week Two section.

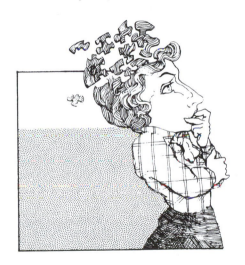

WEEKLY STUDY SCHEDULE

Use the form below to make a schedule for your second week. Use your first week's schedule as a model.

Please follow these steps:
1. Record your class and lab periods.
2. Add your work hours, if any.
3. Fill in the study hours you feel are necessary.

Week of _____							
	Monday	**Tuesday**	**Wednesday**	**Thursday**	**Friday**	**Saturday**	**Sunday**
8:00							
9:00							
10:00							
11:00							
12:00							
1:00							
2:00							
3:00							
4:00							
5:00							
6:00							
7:00							
8:00							
9:00							
10:00							

SECOND WEEK ASSESSMENT

This exercise is a personal progress report. It is designed to help you pinpoint areas of success or areas where renewed emphasis is needed. Complete this assessment only after you have been in a class or classes for two full weeks. Check ☑ the appropriate box. Be totally honest with yourself.

	FULLY SATISFIED	PARTIALLY SATISFIED	NOT SATISFIED
Am I making progress in preparing an effective study schedule?	☐	☐	☐
How is my level of classroom concentration?	☐	☐	☐
Am I becoming a better reader?	☐	☐	☐
Is my note taking improving?	☐	☐	☐
Am I satisfied with my study patterns?	☐	☐	☐
Am I making good use of the campus library?	☐	☐	☐
Am I speaking up enough in the classroom?	☐	☐	☐
Am I making new friends?	☐	☐	☐
Am I sticking with weekly goals?	☐	☐	☐
How do I feel about my overall academic and social progress?	☐	☐	☐

Based on my answers, I intend to concentrate on improving the following areas next week:

1. _____
2. _____
3. _____
4. _____
5. _____

The Classroom
Experience

> Work is what you do so that sometime you
> won't have to do it anymore.
>
> Alfred Polgar

A REMINDER!

As stated earlier, your personal attitude toward learning will be the key to your success in college and in your career. As you enter your third week, a reminder of this may be appropriate. Please complete the following scale. Circle the 10 if you agree 100 percent with the statement. Circle the 1 if you are in total disagreement. Most students fall somewhere in the middle.

You can still learn from a boring prof.	10 9 8 7 6 5 4 3 2 1	It is impossible to learn if the prof is boring.
It's an exciting challenge to learn from a textbook.	10 9 8 7 6 5 4 3 2 1	A textbook is deadly.
Learning is fun.	10 9 8 7 6 5 4 3 2 1	Learning is a bummer.
Asking questions shows a learning attitude.	10 9 8 7 6 5 4 3 2 1	Asking questions shows stupidity.
Learning enhances all aspects of life.	10 9 8 7 6 5 4 3 2 1	There is little payoff to formal learning.
Learning provides inner satisfaction.	10 9 8 7 6 5 4 3 2 1	Learning doesn't turn me on.
Great fulfillment comes from learning.	10 9 8 7 6 5 4 3 2 1	Learning allows one to show off.
I'm here to learn.	10 9 8 7 6 5 4 3 2 1	I'm here to play.
Learning is its own reward.	10 9 8 7 6 5 4 3 2 1	Learning is pressure.
I seek a high GPA for personal and competitive reasons.	10 9 8 7 6 5 4 3 2 1	I want to survive. GPA is not important.

Total _____

A score of 70 or more indicates you have a good learning attitude and college will be a rich and rewarding experience. A score of under 70 indicates you may have a learning block. You should discuss it with a counselor.

HOW PROFESSORS GRADE

True, you are in college to learn, not just to earn the best possible GPA. But because GPA is so important, you should know something about the grading system your professors use. And know ahead of time!

Two of the most popular procedures are:

Point Systems. Some precise, highly organized professors devise their own individual point systems for grading purposes. The typical system applies weights to each examination and each project. A midterm might be worth a maximum of 100 points, and the final exam a maximum of 200 points. Some professors assign points for laboratory work, attendance records, and so on. The system also permits the professor to give short quizzes without assigning letter grades.

An instructor using a point-system approach might wait until the end of the term to decide the cutoff levels for A, B, C, and D letter grades.

The Normal Distribution Curve. Some professors use the traditional bell-shaped curve to determine in advance how many A, B, C, D, and F grades they will give. In a class of twenty students, for example (assuming everyone completes the course), two A, four B, eight C, four D and two F grades might be given. Some professors allow variations.

You need to know in advance what grading system to expect so that you can make your course analysis and plan accordingly. Feel free to raise this subject in class.

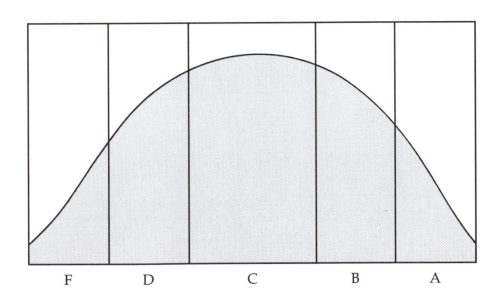

PSYCHING OUT PROFS

College professors come in all sizes, shapes, and types. It is as important to read them properly as it is to read your textbooks. If you are lucky, most instructors will be easy to know from the start. But a few might throw you a curve until you get to know them better. Here are a few "prof profiles" to show you what to expect.

The Shake-Out Artist. This type may ask you to look around the room at your fellow students, with the dismal prediction that half of those present will have departed before the end of the term. Don't be intimidated!

The Sandbagger. This is the professor who starts out so quietly that you think you have a snap course—only to discover the direct opposite later. Don't be taken in!

The Fuddy-Duddy. Here we have a professor who is devoted to the smallest of details. Little things will often count more than they should. To protect yourself, adjust!

The Beautiful Orator. A few talented professors have perfected the lecture method of teaching. They lull you into enjoying their presentations so much that you forget to take notes and study the text. Don't let this occur!

There are two fundamental factors to consider:

1. Reading, analyzing, interpreting, and adjusting to your professors should be considered part of your college learning experience. Don't fight them, join them. Otherwise you will only victimize yourself.

2. Students usually learn more from teachers they like. In other words, *learn to like your professors* so you can learn from them. Ignore any strange mannerisms or irritating habits they may have.

HANDLING COLLEGE PRESSURES

Sometimes, usually around the third or fourth week, pressures begin to build. Students may feel as if they are in a vice. At other times, they may feel like a block of granite that everybody (especially professors) is chiseling away at. College and stress go together.

Academic Pressures

Some college pressures are generated by demands of the educational institution. In order to stay in college, you must meet project deadlines, make oral reports, and pass examinations. Some typical problems are too little time to study, not knowing how to study, fear of speaking up, and the inability to concentrate, express oneself, or plan ahead.

How can you keep the pressure from hurting you? How can you avoid becoming too tense and frantic? Here are three suggestions:

1. Stick as close as possible to your regular study and work schedule. Avoid late hours. Get some extra work done, but get enough sleep to avoid the tension merry-go-round that spins some students into a state of chaos.

2. Avoid stimulants. Stay away from excessive coffee and drugs that keep you awake but destroy your ability to think clearly and logically when you need to.

3. Assume an air of detachment from the whole crazy rat race.

Personal Pressures

Other pressures result from psychological needs and social relationships. Along with the desire for acceptance, students may experience lack of self-confidence, loneliness, awkwardness in meeting others, and difficulty in getting along with parents or roommates. Some students are troubled by weight problems, sex problems, moodiness, inability to relax, or general dissatisfaction with their own personalities.

What should you do if you have a personal problem that has taken priority over academic matters? What should you do if you find yourself so troubled that you can no longer concentrate on your class work?

Yell for help!

Walk into the guidance or student activities office of your campus and ask to see a counselor or advisor for *personal counseling*. Approach this office just as you would walk into a medical clinic if you were ill. Don't hesitate. Don't talk yourself into thinking you can handle it on your own. Colleges spend large sums of money to provide their students with professional, personal guidance. Take advantage of it.

TYPICAL ORIENTATION QUESTIONS

> *How important is my college catalog? What other help does it offer besides course descriptions and graduation requirements?*

The catalog should be your first source for answering almost any questions you have. If you check the index, you will find that it contains information about a variety of topics, from parking regulations to scholarships and loans. Often, if the catalog does not have the exact information you need, it will refer you to another source on campus. Take the time right away to become familiar with it—it's chock-full of useful information.

> *At my college we're encouraged to study the catalog, choose our courses, and plan our schedule before we see our advisors. Is this generally the accepted procedure?*

Yes. For several reasons, it is best to explore independently your career possibilities and course selections before you see your advisor. First, since the ultimate choices are yours, the burden of searching belongs on your shoulders. Second, you will understand the possibilities better if you study them ahead of time. Third, the more research and thinking you do on your own in advance, the more help your advisor will be able to provide.

> *How can I save money at the college bookstore?*

(1) Check your bookstore early so that you can buy used textbooks, if available. Make sure they are actually required and basic to your courses. While you are at it, check off-campus book swaps. (2) Do not buy supplemental or recommended books or equipment until after you have attended your first class. Professors sometimes change their minds. (3) Don't overbuy at the beginning. Start out with the bare necessities so that you can make better decisions later.

> *Should I keep records such as tests, receipts, and notes?*

The more the better. There are two reasons for this: (1) Should you wish to pursue a grievance at a later date, what you have in writing may enable you to prove your point. (2) You may need your receipts for income tax purposes. Obviously, you should check with the IRS and your state income tax service.

> *How important are campus rules and regulations?*

Obey the rules, especially parking rules. Many campuses have outside police to monitor their parking facilities and issue tickets. No campus can operate without ground rules.

> *What about saving a distasteful makeup class or an extremely difficult required course for summer session?*

Generally, it's a good idea. Most students achieve better when they can concentrate on a single course. In making your decision, weigh this advantage against your need for a break from college work or making money for the fall term. Also, bear in mind that some summer classes are very intensive. Many students cannot keep up.

> *What about receiving credit by examination, or challenging, a course?*

Most colleges have adopted procedures whereby a qualified student can *challenge* a course by passing an examination in order to receive a grade without attending a single class. If through training, experience, or independent study you feel you can successfully challenge one or more courses, check your catalog or contact the office of the dean of instruction to find out what steps to take. On most campuses a definite procedure is prescribed.

> *Will I really make better decisions if I seek help from my advisor?*

Yes. Getting through college is a long, complicated process, rather like finding your way through a jungle. Many decisions must be made along the way: finding the right career and major, taking the right courses at the right time, and facing a variety of technical problems that are bound to occur. Discussing these problems and decisions with your parents, professors, classmates, and friends is also a good idea, but your advisor is a *professional*. He or she has up-to-date information on academic and career trends and is in the best position to help you find the right direction and to guide you to a safer passage. If you go through the college jungle without your counselor's help, you may become lost and discouraged—and perhaps give up. It is foolish to let that happen.

ORIENTATION QUESTIONS
(Continued)

> *Why do I feel uncomfortable about taking the initiative to see my advisor?*

You may have psychological blocks that cause difficulties in taking the first step. You could be carrying around a mistaken image of advisors caused by a negative experience with a high school counselor. Your personal pride may be overselling you on the idea that you are a mature person now who should be able to make your own decisions. You may feel that an advisor may try to pry into a part of your life you don't wish to share.

Whatever is holding you back from making that initial contact, you owe it to yourself to overcome it. College advisors or counselors are unlike those who work at other levels. Since they are not concerned with discipline problems, you can be sure they will respect the confidentiality of whatever you tell them. If you have a problem regarding a particular instructor, your counselors will, whenever possible, take your side. They won't try to push you in one direction or another, but will simply provide you with all the data available and help you make your own decisions. You'll survive better and benefit from your college experience more fully if you take advantage of the help offered.

> *What if I feel uncomfortable with or lack confidence in my advisor?*

Then by all means seek another advisor. If you have been assigned a permanent advisor, talk to the appointment receptionist or, if necessary, the dean of guidance. Your present counselor is interested in your well-being and will recognize that another advisor may better suit your needs and personality.

> *How can I find out what kind of help is provided by student personnel services?*

Locate and drop by the central office your first week on campus. The receptionist can probably give you a brochure listing their services. Generally speaking, student personnel services include almost everything on campus with the exception of the academic, administrative, and housekeeping functions. In addition to guidance services, the list would probably include student body fees and cards, student insurance, job placement bureau, housing, transportation, campus maps, student government, athletic programs, intramural sports, financial aids (loans and scholarships), campus newpapers and radio stations, health services, and information about concerts and dances. The only way to find out what is available is to investigate.

YOUR ACADEMIC SUPPORT SYSTEM

Academic failure—or near failure—can be a shattering experience. Discovering you may not pass a course steps hard on your self-esteem. If this happened to you, how would you cope? Would you walk away or fight back?

Your best bet is to step back, analyze the reasons for your poor position, and immediately call upon your campus support system for assistance. Your academic support system is usually called a Learning Resource Center. Almost every campus has one. Such centers provide the specific help you need to survive.

In many centers individualized instructional programs are combined with tutorial guidance to provide a balanced instructional program. In other centers, developmental classes are offered by the center itself, rather than the various divisions or disciplines. Learning opportunities are offered in developmental reading, study skills, spelling, vocabulary, writing, basic mathematics, and other subjects offered in the regular curriculum. The classes are always remedial, so that the student can survive in the academic mainstream.

Admitting the need for special help is never easy. Yet frequently survival depends upon it. Some students, rather than face the makeup class route, either drop out of college or change their majors. Both reactions are short-sighted and foolish when professional help is available at no cost.

The key to your success at a learning center is primarily your own attitude. With your persistence and concentration, any handicap you might have can be overcome. But your attitude toward taking a developmental class or makeup course is critical. Here are suggestions.

Noncredit, refresher courses are no picnic. If you take one, you may discover it is just the opposite. These courses are tough because they contain knowledge and fundamentals you didn't get the first time around. If it wasn't easy the first time, naturally it may not be easy the second time.

You may have to overcome a mental block. Because you had trouble learning the subject in the past, you may have what psychologists call a *mental block* against learning it now. This means you are probably afraid of the subject now and think it is more difficult than it really is. Such fears are usually groundless for several reasons:
• You are older now and more ready to learn.
• You have a different and perhaps more capable teacher.
• Your motivation to learn is stronger.

SOURCES OF HELP

Check ☑ Those you anticipate using.

☐ **Career Center**
Go here when you do not have a career goal and fear you may be on the wrong educational track.

☐ **Child Care Center**
Some campuses have free child care centers where young children receive care and training while their parents are in classes.

☐ **Counseling Center**
You are welcome here at all times for academic, clinical, and other forms of guidance.

☐ **Learning Assistance or Developmental Center**
Another name for the learning resource center—the place to go to upgrade your basic skills so you can survive in the academic mainstream.

☐ **Financial Aid Center**
Go here for information on grants, loans, and scholarships.

☐ **Job Placement Bureau**
This office is the place to go for employment, either on or off campus.

☐ **Legal Clinic**
Some larger campuses now provide free legal guidance to students.

☐ **Library**
Most libraries have a short orientation program or a brochure that explains how to use library facilities. Librarians also provide individual assistance.

☐ **Physical Education Center**
Besides credit courses, other programs are available: extracurricular programs, adapted activities for the physically handicapped, and other individualized physical improvement programs.

☐ **Student Health Services**
Major colleges have their own dispensaries and doctor's offices; others provide a nurse for consultation and help.

☐ **Tutorial Services**
Go to the developmental center or the learning resource center.

☐ **Veterans' Center**
Veterans can obtain many kinds of counseling to assist them in successful college careers.

☐ **Women's Center**
Most campuses have special centers to help women make maximum use of educational opportunities. They often support assertive action and affirmative action programs of various kinds.

FINANCIAL SURVIVAL

Money is a problem for most college students. Few deans of admission will say that financial need is the chief cause of college drop-outs, but all conclude it is near the top of the list.

Let's assume that you did not arrive on your campus with a scholarship under your arm and that you will need additional funds to reach your academic goal. What choices are available to you? Here are the three that most students rely on:

- An outright *grant* that need not be paid back
- A *loan* from a government, commercial, or family source
- A *job*

To discover what is available and what is right for you, go to your campus financial center without delay. If you decide to finance your education in whole or in part through a part-time or full-time job, keep the following in mind:

- Most college students work. Those with full-time jobs usually take a partial academic load. Those who take a full academic load (more than 12 units) usually work part-time. Some students work full-time and take a full academic load and get excellent grades.
- The right job can provide a profitable release from the mental fatigue resulting from hard study.
- A job may help you find a career goal.
- Your education should always have first priority.
- If possible, find a job that will complement your education.
- Fit your job schedule into your study schedule, not the other way around.
- If you are taking a full load, limit your work to 20 hours or less per week.

WORK THROUGH YOUR JOB PLACEMENT BUREAU.

WEEKLY STUDY SCHEDULE

This is the third and last study schedule you are encouraged to complete. With two schedules behind you, this one should be the one you follow for the rest of the term. It should be your model, so give it your best effort.

	Monday	Tuesday	Wednesday	Thursday	Friday	Saturday	Sunday
Week of _____							
8:00							
9:00							
10:00							
11:00							
12:00							
1:00							
2:00							
3:00							
4:00							
5:00							
6:00							
7:00							
8:00							
9:00							
10:00							

CASE PROBLEMS

Read each case and write out your answer. Then compare your answers with the author's suggestions on pages 77-78.

Case 12. Gil arrived on campus highly motivated, but he has slowly drifted into poor study habits. For the last three days he hasn't opened a book, although he is behind both on reading assignments and basic projects. He decides he will set aside eight hours every Saturday for the rest of the semester for what he calls "pressure study." He will go to the campus library and sweat it out under intense pressure from himself. As a reward, he is offering himself a special dune buggy trip each Sunday—providing he accomplishes enough to meet his own standards.

Will the system work? _____

_____

_____

Case 13. Sally, a business administration major, is constantly irritated by her accounting teacher, Mrs. Long. The teacher's voice is loud and raspy. She has a nervous laugh, and she frequently refuses to answer questions. Her brusque impatience is humiliating to those who need more time to learn. The situation has become so disturbing that Sally is finding it difficult to concentrate in class. As a result, she is not doing well on the frequent tests.

Should she drop the class? _____

_____

_____

Case 14. Alice is a rather quiet, reserved freshman who spends almost all her spare time studying. Her parents pay all her expenses and give her a weekly allowance. She is thinking about seeking a four-year college degree, but she has no definite career goal. Her grades in high school were average. Her father recently advised: "Devote all of your time to getting better grades, Alice. You will have the rest of your life to work." Yesterday one of her friends told her about an interesting fifteen-hour-per-week job within walking distance of her home.

Should Alice apply for the job? _____

_____

_____

Case 15. Shannon feels as if she has been on a crazy merry-go-round ever since she arrived at the university two months ago. She doesn't remember exactly how her merry-go-round started but she's been whirling through one caper after another with drugs, alcohol—the works. At first she was intoxicated with her new freedom, but now she feels used and frightened and has fallen hopelessly behind in her classes. Can she make it through the semester? What will her parents say? Yesterday she gathered up her courage and had a long talk with her college advisor who suggested that Shannon pull away from her present friends and accept special tutoring.

Do you think this will save her? _____

_____

_____

THIRD WEEK ASSESSMENT

Complete this assessment only after you have been in a class or classes for three weeks. Check the appropriate box. Be totally honest with yourself.

	FULLY SATISFIED	PARTIALLY SATISFIED	NOT SATISFIED
Am I making enough progress on my individual course strategies?	☐	☐	☐
Am I figuring out my profs?	☐	☐	☐
Do I understand their grading systems?	☐	☐	☐
What about my study schedule?	☐	☐	☐
Am I satisfied with progress on my learning attitude?	☐	☐	☐
Am I balancing my studies with enough fun and exercise?	☐	☐	☐
Am I taking advantage of all campus support?	☐	☐	☐
Have I built a good relationship with my counselor?	☐	☐	☐
How satisfied am I with my first three weeks on campus?	☐	☐	☐
Do I have the right balance between home, work, leisure, and academic program?	☐	☐	☐

Based on my answers, I intend to concentrate on improving the following areas next week:

1. _____

2. _____

3. _____

4. _____

5. _____

WEEK FOUR

Preparing for Exams

All of us learn to write in the second grade ...
most of us go on to greater things.

Bobby Knight

THE FOURTH WEEK SLUMP

I keep hearing about a third or fourth week slump. Is there such a thing?

For most students, yes. An air of excitement usually surrounds the first few weeks of college, lifting your spirits and sweeping you into an atmosphere of exhilaration. Most new students enjoy responding to this new climate.

Then, as you settle into campus life, you may experience a letdown feeling that leaves you tired and depressed. You may find yourself staring at your books, avoiding your assignments, and looking ahead with fear.

What can you do? You can react in one of three ways. First, you can make a desperate but foolish attempt to seek more nonacademic involvements to keep the air of excitement alive. Second, you can do nothing and let the slump drown you in your own self-pity. Third, and most advisable, you can pick up your books and begin to study with dedication. If you accept the challenge of learning, a different kind of excitement will soon surround you. To get out of the slump, you must provide your own lifesaver.

Sometimes loneliness accompanies a slump. Loneliness is a feeling of complete isolation. It is four walls crowding in on you. It is despair. Loneliness can occur at any age and in many situations. It is nothing to be ashamed of; it is a normal human emotion. But loneliness presents a special problem for college freshmen, especially those who have left their homes and communities. It has a way of creeping up on them without warning. When this happens, their minds are jolted away from their studies. It is a serious malady. If you don't fight it off quickly, it can destroy your college career.

The only way to fight loneliness successfully is to build new relationships with the people around you—those who are accessible. You can't replace your relationships with those you miss, but you can substitute. Writing letters and making frequent long-distance telephone calls may bridge the gap temporarily; but only new, worthwhile relationships will eliminate loneliness. Move beyond the four walls of your room. Take the initiative and make new friends. Talk to those students who sit next to you in class. Study in the library where it is easier to meet people. Attend social events. At the beginning of each school year, many campus clubs solicit membership. Consider joining one.

Loneliness is a tough enemy to fight—your only ammunition is to meet new people. If you withdraw further into yourself, loneliness will cover you like a blanket and your survival will be doubtful.

INSIDE CONTRACTS

As a college student, you will soon discover that you can't expect others to motivate you. A few inspirational professors, advisors, and tutors may encourage you, but motivation on campus is primarily a do-it-yourself affair.

Sometimes you will need to reach inside yourself to get going. Nobody is going to push you through a library door, design a study schedule that fits your needs, or lead you to a professor's office for consultation. On a typical campus you'll be tempted to relax and enjoy some of the nonacademic activities and develop special relationships with others. Great, as long as you balance nonacademic activities with the primary reason you are on campus in the first place. To learn!

On any campus there are many goal-oriented students with "inside contracts" that they do not always talk about. They aspire to be on the dean's academic list. They want a GPA that will protect a scholarship. Like others, these individuals have temporary "down periods," but their goals are so important that such periods last only a short time.

What about you? How can you motivate and discipline yourself? How can you create an inner contract that will work? Here are two suggestions:

1. Use the delayed-gratification theory (see page 8). Expecting a simple but important reward *after something has been accomplished* can provide the stimulus you need.

> Phil is a "disco nut" whose greatest pleasure is dancing. But Phil has a tough contract with himself. He must complete a premed program and hold down a 24-hour part-time job each week. Solution? He grinds out work all week knowing he can reward himself on Saturday night at a local disco.

2. Use the psychological advantage theory. Learn how to benefit from a negative situation by turning things around so you have the advantage.

> Trix found herself in a required class that was very boring. Looking around, she noticed her fellow students were turning the professor off and learning very little. The next day she made an appointment to meet the professor. She made an effort to understand him better. Result? She changed her attitude, started speaking up in class, and decided to learn enough to get an A grade.

SHOULD YOU DROP A COURSE?

Dropping a course is a major decision! It is usually a downer. It can delay your progress and depress your attitude. Still, there are times when it is a smart decision. If you are thinking about dropping a course, look at the drop decision scale below. It can help you make the best decision for your future. Circle where you think you fall on the scale for the course you are thinking about dropping.

If I want to, I can fully motivate myself to complete this course.	5 4 3 2 1	There is no possible way to motivate myself to complete it.
I have all the time I need to make up any back work required.	5 4 3 2 1	I'm strapped for time; that's the reason I'm in trouble.
I am capable of handling the work, or I'm willing to accept tutoring.	5 4 3 2 1	The course is over my head and I refuse tutoring even if it is free.
I recognize I am learning and making progress.	5 4 3 2 1	The course is meaningless; I'm wasting my time.
I really like the teacher's dedication and style.	5 4 3 2 1	The teacher is the main reason I want out.
I'm not under any outside pressure—financial or personal.	5 4 3 2 1	I'm under impossible pressures.
This course is vital to my career goal.	5 4 3 2 1	The course is not related to my career goal.
I can be happy with a C or passing grade.	5 4 3 2 1	Only an A grade is acceptable in this course.

Total Score _____

If you rated yourself 30 or over, it is a signal you should continue with the course. If you rated yourself under 20, it is a signal you should consult with the professor and your guidance counselor before making a final decision.

HOW TO TAKE EXAMS

BE PREPARED AND THEN SAVE TIME FOR REVIEW. Train yourself to prepare in a steady, organized manner throughout the term. Then you can use your last few study hours to rethink and review the material already covered. The purpose of reviewing is to fit all the small pieces into the overall picture. This helps you recall them during the examination. Cramming eliminates this important review time.

GET TOGETHER WITH OTHER STUDENTS AND QUIZ EACH OTHER.

ARRIVE EARLY FOR THE EXAM SO THAT YOU CAN MAINTAIN YOUR COMPOSURE. Any nervousness you already have will increase if you arrive hot, flustered, and barely on time. It is better to be comfortable and ready when the professor arrives. Be sure to have an extra pen with you as well as other required materials.

FOLLOW THIS PROCEDURE IN TAKING OBJECTIVE TESTS:
1. Determine how many different kinds of items are used: true-false, multiple choice, matching, and the like. Read directions carefully and ask questions if you are confused. Find out whether there is a penalty for guessing.
2. Answer the easier questions first. If you struggle with the difficult questions as you go along, you may become frustrated and bogged down.
3. When you begin work on the hard questions, check to see how much time you have left and allocate it among the remaining items.

FOLLOW THIS PROCEDURE IN TAKING ESSAY EXAMINATIONS:
1. Take a good look at the entire examination and then pace yourself to answer each section. Allocate your time evenly. Don't make the mistake of leaving too little time to answer the last questions. Some students wisely assign time quotas to each question and note them in the margin before they proceed with the examination.
2. Scan each question once and then read it more carefully a second time, underlining key words. Be sure you understand the full meaning of the question before you proceed. More students than you would suspect do poorly on examinations because they hastily misinterpret the questions.
3. In answering broad, subjective questions, sketch a quick outline before you write out the full answer. This will help you organize your thoughts and save time in the long run. Remember—it's not how much you say but *what* you say and *how* you say it that counts. You'll improve your score if you spend more time thinking and less time answering.
4. You are graded by what you have written, not by what is in your mind. Your instructor cannot give you credit for what you have learned if he cannot read what you have said. Use a good pen and write legibly. Watch your spelling and sentence structure. Use examples and diagrams to communicate.

RESEARCH PAPERS

Many professors require sophisticated written themes, projects, or research papers from their students. Sometimes a substantial part of the final course grade is tied to such an effort. Consider this kind of assignment as an opportunity to express your thoughts in a creative manner, not as a hurdle that will send you into a state of confusion and frustration. Accept it as a challenge.

BEGIN EARLY BY SELECTING A TITLE AND TOPIC. Start your preparation as soon as you receive the assignment.

GO TO THE LIBRARY AND DO SOME READING ON YOUR TOPIC. Gather some facts. Explore a variety of sources. When you find something of value that is pertinent, write it down carefully and record the source (the author, title, date, and publisher). You may wish to use this data later in preparing footnotes or a bibliography. Many students prefer to use 3″ × 5″ notecards to record data. It's usually helpful to jot down in the upper right or left corner the topic of the information on each card. This step can save much rereading and reshuffling of the cards later.

PREPARE A GENERAL OUTLINE. Very few people can write about a complex topic without an outline. In preparing an outline, think of an introduction, body, and conclusion; then divide the body into three or four major headings. Under each heading write out the specific points that illustrate and support it, based on your research. After you have begun writing, you may wish to revise your outline from time to time.

WRITE OUT THE FIRST DRAFT. Sit down for two or three hours and write. Use your research notes. Stay away from long, complicated sentences. Don't worry too much at this stage about mechanical errors such as punctuation and misspelled words. The important step here is to get your ideas down on paper according to your basic outline.

REVISE THE FIRST DRAFT, PROOFREAD IT, AND THEN TYPE IT.

When your project is returned by your professor, take the time to go over your errors. If you don't understand all the comments or want more feedback, see your instructor for a more detailed critique. If you do not learn from your mistakes, the instructor is wasting his time making corrections and suggestions, and you will find yourself making the same errors over and over again.

ORAL REPORTS

How do you feel about standing in front of your classmates and talking? Are you comfortable about giving a ten-minute oral report with or without notes? If you are very clever in selecting your courses and professors, you may be able to eliminate this problem. You might avoid public speaking classes and professors who think verbal communication on your feet is important. If you get caught, you can always drop the class in a hurry.

This approach would enable you to relax and concentrate on taking tests and writing papers. *It would also be a serious mistake.*

Sometime in your life you will probably have to give talks as a part of your career or community life. Why not learn how to it *now* in a friendly atmosphere where the penalty is not so great? Face the challenge. You will probably find that any mental block you may have against such an experience will slowly crumble. Here are some tips that might help:

GET EXCITED OVER YOUR TOPIC. If you can choose your own subject, select one that you know a great deal about—something that you find intriguing and exciting.

USE THE RULE OF THREE. Write out your talk in advance and center it in three main points. Not two or four—but three. (If you find it difficult to narrow your report to three points, you are probably trying to cover too much.) Memorize these three points, organizing your speech around them.

GIVE THE TALK TO YOURSELF. Talk to yourself standing in front of a mirror. If possible, tape-record it and play it back.

LOOK SHARP AND EXPECT BUTTERFLIES. Anyone who has to stand up in front of his fellow students is nervous—so look sharp. Wear your best campus outfit. Feeling good about your appearance gives you additional confidence when you feel your classmates' eyes on you.

BE YOURSELF. Don't try to fake it. You are who you are; speak, smile, and gesture in your natural way. You can't communicate your ideas if you deny your own personality and try to be different from what you are.

NEVER APOLOGIZE. Don't downgrade yourself by making excuses either at the beginning or the end of your talk.

64

CASE PROBLEMS

Read each case and write out your answer. Then compare your answers with the author's suggestions on page 78.

Case 16. Sylvia has wanted to become a veterinarian or physician since she was twelve years old. Every test she has taken has reinforced this dream. When she entered college three months ago, she was advised to take chemistry and advanced algebra. But last week both her chemistry and math professors told her that her work was less than satisfactory. Sylvia was so discouraged that she dropped both courses.

Did she take the right action? _____

_____

_____

Case 17. Raoul is an excellent science student. He saved a lot of money during the summer after graduating from high school. He has enough money to survive his first year without accepting any help from his parents. But he knows that at some point he will run into money problems because he plans to go to graduate school. He has thought about finding a part-time job, but his science labs usually keep him on campus until late in the afternoon. He also realizes that he must do well in all his first-year courses in order to build a good foundation for later advanced courses. Yesterday Raoul was offered a job as an ambulance driver on Saturday and Sunday nights from 4 p.m. to midnight.

Should he take it? _____

_____

_____

Case 18. Margo is in her early thirties. She was recently divorced and has two children. She enrolled in college to become a teacher and wants to take every possible shortcut toward getting her credential. To support herself and her family, she must work part-time while attending college. A highly assertive woman, she explains her attitude in this way: "I am here to earn my degree and my credential and then find a teaching job. Nothing else matters. I haven't the time to build relationships with other students or teachers. I'm going to do the academic work and that's all."

Is Margo making a good decision? _____

_____

_____

Case 19. Sid is a serious, full-time engineering student on the right educational track and moving at a sound pace. He knows, however, that he will run short of money this semester if he keeps on spending so much on his girlfriend. She likes expensive entertainment and is becoming more demanding.

What should Sid do? _____

_____

_____

FOURTH WEEK ASSESSMENT

You have completed a personal assessment on your progress for each of the last three weeks. Now it is time for a different, more rewarding kind of assessment or appraisal. It is recommended that you talk over your first four weeks with a significant other. This can be a close friend, spouse, college advisor, mentor, or anyone interested in your future.

In doing this, consider discussing these questions:

How do you feel about your college experience so far?
What has been your most rewarding experience?
Has there been a low point?
What about the rest of the term?
What about future long-range plans?

Talking over these questions with the right person could help reinforce what you have learned and could help you crystallize your thoughts for the future.

In addition to talking things over, you might enjoy testing yourself on what you have learned. If so, complete the self-quiz on the following page.

DEMONSTRATE YOUR PROGRESS

To measure how well you have learned the techniques and principles of this book, please answer the following questions. Correct answers will be found on the next page.

True False

1. In preparing a research paper, it is a mistake to worry about a title at the beginning.

2. In a long, difficult exam, it is a mistake to answer the easy questions first.

3. If you have not had time to prepare a good oral report, start out with an apology.

4. There is no such thing as a fourth week slump.

5. DG stands for Delayed Gratification.

6. There is a close relationship between one's attitude and how much one learns.

7. Only a few students graduate knowing they took the wrong major.

8. For students who do not have a clear career goal, a serious career exploration should be undertaken as soon as possible.

9. Those who listen with their eyes as well as their ears are usually better listeners.

10. The Record-and-Condense method is a recommended technique for taking notes.

11. The Press-Stress theory is a technique for taking exams.

12. The Rule of Three technique is a good way to read a chapter.

13. If a new student prepares a study schedule the first week, it will last the entire term.

14. It is best to study before, instead of after, a lecture.

15. When attempting to improve your reading speed it is okay to use your finger as a pacer.

16. Students who take time to analyze each course and professor usually wind up with the best grades.

17. Both math and shorthand are examples of constant-discipline courses.

18. History is a good example of a delayed-action course.

19. Chemistry is an example of a self-involving course.

20. All professors are required to use the same system in determining grades.

_____ _____ 21. A sandbagger is a professor whose beginning bark is worse than her bite.

_____ _____ 22. It's better to drop a class than to accept a free tutor.

_____ _____ 23. All financial grants must be paid back.

_____ _____ 24. Most college students who take a full academic load (12 units) do not work as well.

_____ _____ 25. Academic freedom means you can skip classes as often as you wish.

Total Correct _____

REPLAY!

If you discover at the end of your first thirty days on campus that you are not doing as well academically as you had anticipated—perhaps barely surviving—a replay of this book is in order. In other words, go back to Week One and start over. Under these circumstances, Week One will become Week Five, Week Two will become Week Six, and so on.

IT IS NEVER TOO LATE TO PUT
THE TECHNIQUES OF THIS BOOK
INTO PRACTICE.

ANSWERS

1. F (A good title can help create a better paper.)

2. F (Answering easy questions first can provide confidence and get more questions answered.)

3. F (An apology will downgrade what you have to say.)

4. F (Slumps are common after three or four weeks.)

5. T

6. T

7. F (According to some estimates, more than 50 percent of students graduate knowing that they took the wrong major.)

8. T (A good time to start is after your thirty day adjustment is complete.)

9. T (Their concentration on what is being said is better.)

10. T

11. F (It is a theory that helps one read more in less time.)

12. T

13. F (A few adjustments are recommended.)

14. F (Going over a lecture while it is fresh in your mind is recommended because you reinforce what you have learned and textbook material means more.)

15. T

16. T

17. T

18. T

19. F

20. F

21. T

22. F

23. F

24. F (Some work full-time; many work part-time.)

25. F (Academic freedom means that professors can teach without interference from government or other officials.)

UNFINISHED BUSINESS

Summary

The object of education is to prepare the young
to educate themselves throughout their lives.
Robert Maynard Hutchins

KNOWING YOURSELF BETTER

Two university counselors, over coffee, were discussing how to start career interviews. One said, ''I used to come right out and ask students if they knew what they wanted to do. Now I ask if they *know themselves well enough* to make such a tough decision.''

The difference is significant.

The more you know and understand yourself—your special characteristics—the more college will mean to you, the more you can take advantage of opportunities that surround you, the more success you will have academically now and with your life in general later.

You will, of course, get to know yourself better by attending classes, reacting to others, doing research, and becoming involved in other activities. But there is a more direct route.

Take advantage of some of the tests and inventories designed to help you know yourself better. You'll be able to make better career and lifestyle decisions.

What is available? Where do you go to take them? Are they expensive? Will taking one embarrass you?

There are four general kinds of tests available on most campuses through the counseling office or career center:

- *Achievement Tests.* These can measure your ability to learn and achieve. Not everyone can be a research scientist, for example.
- *Interest Inventories.* When you know your high interests, you can often choose a major academic track that will lead you to careers you will enjoy more.
- *Special Aptitude Tests.* If you are thinking about becoming a programmer, you could take the Computer Programmer Aptitude Battery. This will tell you if you have ability in this direction.
- *Personality Profiles.* Properly interpreted by a professional, these can furnish considerable insight.

Most tests take around an hour to complete. Computer scoring may require you to wait a week or so for the results. A modest charge is usually involved. Making and keeping appointments to take such tests and have them interpreted requires careful scheduling.

If you are like most people, you have a tendency to put off seeking professional guidance on campus. False pride or fear is often at the bottom of such procrastination. Remember that *all* students can benefit, and most students require some kind of on-campus guidance.

The longer you delay, the less success you can expect!

SELECTING A MAJOR

Whatever else you attempt in college, do everything possible to get on the right educational track so you graduate with the right major. Here are two of many reasons:

- Your career choices are tied closely to your college major. If you get on the wrong track now, many excellent career opportunities may be closed to you later.
- Knowing you are on the right track will help give you the motivation to graduate. Interviews indicate that many college dropouts were unable to find a major of sufficient interest to keep them motivated.

Two things you need to know at the beginning: (1) Some colleges require you to declare a major not later than your junior year. (2) Although assistance is available, it is a decision you eventually must make on your own.

To help you get started in the selection of an academic major, you are encouraged to complete the college major preference profile in the appendix.

Keep in mind, choosing a career and an academic major are the two most critical decisions you will make in college.

CAREER EXPLORATION

Have you done a serious career exploration? Do you know the career cluster where you belong? If not, as soon as you have completed your first thirty days, visit your career center or enroll in a career exploration class. You must discover what you hope to do with your life so that you can get on the right academic track as soon as possible.

Otherwise, you may incur two major disadvantages:

1. You may prolong your college days unnecessarily, because the courses you take may not lead to a valid career goal.

2. If you do not find a motivating career goal, your chances of dropping out of college are *doubled*.

Many campuses have one- or two-unit courses designed to help students establish or set career goals. Such courses are highly recommended for the following reasons:

• The working world is more sophisticated today. The more help you get the better.
• Career planning is more complicated. Working with the support of a professional guidance person is often necessary.
• Psychological factors are more complex. Certain inventories, psychological instruments, and computer systems can help you find the right track to take.

You have one additional option you may wish to take instead of enrolling in a course. Go to your career center and ask for individual help. For example, the author of this book has written a well-researched book called *Career Discovery*. It is available in many Career Centers—or it can be ordered direct from the publisher.* It is a do-it-yourself program that can provide immediate results.

Career Discovery, published by Crisp Publications, can be ordered using the form at the back of this book.

CASE PROBLEMS

Read each case and write out your answer. The author's comments are on page 79.

Case 20. Bruce enrolled at a local college primarily because he wanted to discover what to do with his life. His plan was simple: he would take a single course in every possible department or division until he found one that he really liked. Only then would he start concentrating on one area. He decided that his plan would eventually lead him to a good career, although he admitted that it would take some extra time.

Do you approve of Bruce's plan? _____

_____

_____

Case 21. Angela took an interest inventory, talked with her counselor at length, and did considerable research on her own. She became convinced that she wanted to spend her life helping others. She finally narrowed her choice to three careers: teaching, social work, and personnel work in business. Her planned strategy is first to get a credential and try to become a teacher. If that doesn't work, she will then try social work. If nothing opens up there, she will seek a position is business that will lead to personnel work.

Is Angela's strategy sound? _____

_____

_____

Case 22. Chin is a sophomore. He wants to be an educated person and is not concerned about career goals at this stage of his life. He wants broad educational background with emphasis on the humanities. As he puts it: "It's foolish for me to worry about a career now. First, I need to find myself and my values. Later, after I earn my degree, there will be plenty of time to worry about a career."

*Do you agree with Chin?*_____

_____

_____

Case 23. Juan is a quiet, reserved freshman attending college on a small but helpful scholarship. He is doing well in all his courses but is having trouble making friends. Often he feels as if he's just a bystander, not really a part of campus life. He has discovered that after giving his best effort to his homework, he still has spare time and usually becomes bored. Yesterday Juan noticed that the college bookstore was looking for a stock person to work two hours every afternoon. He considered it briefly, thinking he would like the experience and the money. But he decided not to apply because it might jeopardize his scholarship and hurt him academically.

Did he make the right decision? _____

_____

_____

FUTURE READING

You can read this book in fifty minutes. If you do nothing else, your chances of academic survival in a single class or a four-year college program are measurably improved. You will be a winner! But this book has another advantage. It can lead you to seven additional career and guidance books critical to your future. All are closely related to your college survival and career choices. These popular Crisp publications and the specific purpose of each volume are listed on the following page. You may wish to add one or all of these books to your personal library.

SUPPLEMENTARY READING

These books, also published by Crisp Publications, are helpful for college students:

How to Succeed in College.   Broader in scope than *The College Experience.* Excellent for freshmen planning a four-year program.

Get Your A out of College.   Master the hidden rules of the ''game'' of college. Learn how to get through school with top grades without being frustrated or wasting time. Tips, analysis, and checklists for memorizing, raising test scores, reading textbooks, doing assignments, and much more are included in this best-selling book.

Study Skills Strategies.   Used by more than 200 colleges, this book contains exercises, questions, tips, and self-tests that help a reader develop a good attitude toward studying. Specific topics include note taking skills, time management, memory techniques, exam strategies and much more. It includes information on critical thinking and mathematical study skills. A refreshing, time-saving, inexpensive way to acquire quality study skills.

I Got the Job!   Concentrating on attitude and self-image as the critical ingredients in any job search, this book provides the organizational techniques needed to find and win the best possible job. Case studies, sample resumes and letters, and a wide range of checklists help keep a job applicant positive and motivated.

Career Discovery.   ''Success is finding the right career the first time'' and this book helps a reader do just that. Pick up a pencil and complete the series of tested exercises that will help you discover career possibilities within your ability and comfort zone and which relate to your life goals.

Plan B: Protecting your Career From the Winds of Change.   In this age of mergers, acquisitions, downsizing, and golden handshakes, everyone needs a ''Plan B.'' This readable book is a positive primer for keeping your job skills sharp and yourself marketable. Exercises, case studies, and checklists provide a step-by-step practical process to help you be prepared for the ''winds of change.''

Be True to Your Future.   A combination of the three titles listed above, this book will help to give you direction both as a student and as career planner.

All of the above publications (and others) can be ordered using the order form at the back of this book.

AUTHOR'S COMMENTS ON CASE PROBLEMS

1. Rod. No, he's not making the right decision. Nothing in the case indicates that Rod doesn't need the course. Age and business experience have little to do with academic success, and the overconfidence he shows could be dangerous. Accepting some help with study skills and time management at the beginning could save him time and mistakes and might help him achieve a higher academic standard with less effort. Especially since the course is only six hours, Rod appears to be taking an unnecessary and foolish gamble with his chances of survival.

2. Joyce. Her solution is much better than going to the other extreme—spending all of her time making friends. But along with her academic achievements, she needs to make more effort to communicate with fellow students. She might, for example, seek another student to study with, or she might investigate the possibility of taking an affirmative action workshop for women. Academic achievement alone will not prepare Joyce adequately for whatever career she intends to pursue after she completes her formal education.

3. Jim. Yes, he should enroll in college. Jim's long-range potential, whether in mathematics or music, is much too high for him to shortchange himself by avoiding college. Besides, he is apparently becoming somewhat disenchanted with his present situation. It is quite feasible for him to go to college and keep a rock group going at the same time.

4. Linda. She has a good chance to succeed because one goal complements the other. As she loses weight (success that can be measured) her enthusiasm can spur her on to her second goal, higher academic achievement. If Linda can reach her weight goal by Christmas, her motivation level may be much higher the second semester because of a better self-image. College is a good place to learn self-discipline.

5. Toby. No. Toby needs at least one or two regular credit courses to give himself a feeling of accomplishment and to test his ability to compete with all students. It would be too discouraging to take only makeup classes. Toby would probably be more successful with a more balanced schedule.

6. Martha. No. Many books contain excellent reading improvement techniques but Martha would get better results from the highly professional help she can get in the class. Besides, many reading improvement programs have special equipment not available elsewhere.

AUTHOR'S COMMENTS (Continued)

7. Jack. By all means. More grants and loans are available—eligibility requirements change—some grants and scholarships are not related to income, status, or background. As long as Jack is serious about his education, he should take advantage of any financial opportunities for which he can qualify.

8. Tony. No. Tony cannot fully cover himself unless he attends class on a regular basis. Professor Bush might start covering additional material not found in any available text. Tony's friend might forget to tell him about an important examination or change of schedule. Tony might not be able to discipline himself to use his library time as well as he anticipates. He would do better to work ahead and challenge Mr. Bush by asking questions that might break the monotony.

9. Judy. Yes. If Judy can establish herself as an independent person, various financial support programs may be available to her. When in doubt, investigate. On the other hand, she should not eliminate the possibility of help from her mother or father. Parents do not divorce their children.

10. Terri. No. Marrying Hal at this time could be primarily a means of escape from some problems Terri should face and solve. She needs to search for a career goal and allow college to help her become a stronger person before she seriously considers marriage. Besides, Terri probably could not qualify for a very satisfying job at this point. She might eventually feel used and trapped.

11. Mario. Not if he really wishes to succeed. Mario may need to spend extra time in his college learning center. If he is willing to accept tutoring or take some remedial courses, ultimately he will be able to use his maturity, motivation, and experience to advantage. Being bilingual will be an advantage to him both as a student and as a manager.

12. Gil. It might work, providing Gil is the kind of person who can study only under self-pressure. Many experienced students would say, however, that it would not work. They would say Gil is geared to a pleasure concept and would most likely get sidetracked and lose his concentration.

13. Sally. No. Accounting is a very important class for Sally. She should train herself to look beyond Mrs. Long's irritating mannerisms and keep her mind on the lectures themselves. If she can ignore Mrs. Long's personality and learn to live with her style, Sally will be able to bring her test scores back up and learn the subject matter. If she is already measurably behind, she should consider an appointment with Mrs. Long and possibly tutoring at the learning center.

14. Alice. Yes. It is foolish for Alice to try to use all her spare time for studying when a few hours of work could provide her with relaxation and motivation. The monotony of studying will eventually turn Alice against her educational plan. A balance will maintain her interest. An exposure to the work environment might also increase her self-confidence and help her find a career goal. By working now Alice could start building a financial cushion for the future.

15. Shannon. No. It appears that Shannon has become so deeply involved and lost so much time that she is beyond surviving this term. She should leave the university and seek professional help to work through her problems. Later, when she feels ready, she should enroll at another school and make a fresh start. Many highly successful college students recover from a poor beginning.

Shannon should also talk with her parents. They will probably appreciate her mature decision. Shannon will need their support to resume an educational plan later.

16. Sylvia. No. It would appear that Sylvia gave up too easily. She should have evaluated her study habits, sought some tutorial help, and tried harder to survive. If she didn't succeed the first time, she should consider taking a remedial course and trying again later. If she can conquer these courses, the careers she wants are still possible; if not, she must investigate other alternatives.

17. Raoul. Yes. Raoul might profit from the job in several ways: (1) It would help him financially. (2) It would give him an exposure to the medical field which would be valuable if he later pursues a career in that area. (3) It would provide him with a change of pace without jeopardizing his course schedule. He could even study on some nights when fewer calls are coming in.

18. Margo. No. Margo's attitude may invoke antagonism from her fellow students and make the classroom situation difficult for her teachers. This negative atmosphere is bound to influence her learning environment. Whether she admits it or not, she needs acceptance just as much as anyone else. She should also realize that if she is going to become a teacher, she must begin to develop a sensitivity toward and understanding of younger people.

19. Sid. He should talk things over openly with his girlfriend now, before he gets into trouble that will throw him off his educational track. If she is not understanding, then a choice must be made between his girlfriend and his educational goal.

AUTHOR'S COMMENTS (Continued)

20. Bruce. Yes, Bruce has a good basic plan. But exploring career possibilities by simply taking one course after another is not enough. He should also take some psychological tests, use other career guidance materials, and talk to various professors to speed up the process. He should avoid taking classes that are obviously not suited to him. The Career Tree Exercise, for example, might give Bruce an indication of the courses he should consider taking. Such a step would be much better than just taking courses at random.

21. Angela. Yes. Angela is wise to direct her education toward more than one career goal. Students who follow only one goal often face disappointments when nothing is available in that field. By keeping three options open, Angela will have greater flexibility to follow the available opportunities after she completes her formal education. She should keep in mind, however, that the qualifications for these three careers differ. She might need further training when she moves from one field to another.

22. Chin. No. He is to be admired for wanting to become an educated person, but for at least two reasons he should do some career searching along the way. (1) He may be forced to choose a college major for his junior and senior years. It would be advantageous if he chose one that could lead him to an appropriate career area later. (2) Searching now, while he is on campus and can have concerned professional help, might save him frustrations and disappointments later.

23. Juan. No. Juan should have investigated to find out whether working would affect his scholarship. If it didn't, he should have applied for the job. Working in the bookstore could be very beneficial. He would probably make some new and needed friends; he would have a change of pace during his spare time; and he could earn additional money to supplement his scholarship.

"BALANCING COLLEGE AND WORK IS NO EASY TRICK."

College Major
Preference Profile

Have you scheduled courses in the right acadamic departments?

Are you starting out taking the right subjects?

Are you headed in the right direction?

This exercise will help you select and verify your choices.

PROFILE SHEET

COLLEGE MAJORS

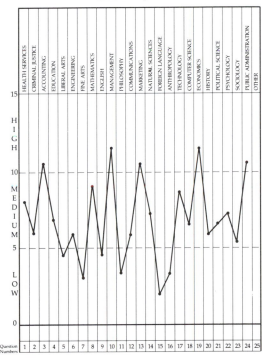

FINDING THE RIGHT TRACK

Selecting the right college major is something like finding the right train in a busy station. In choosing the right train you must know ahead of time where the track will eventually take you. In choosing the right major (getting on the right academic track) you must consider the careers that track may lead you to. If you get on the wrong track, you will discover that you have prepared for the wrong careers. For example, if you don't get on the mathematics track, many careers (physicist or statistician, for example) will not be available to you once the academic journey has been completed.

The exercise that follows is designed to help you start the process of selecting a college major. The right choice will lead you to the careers that best fit with your special desires, values, and personality. Think of the exercise as a ''starter set'' that will introduce you to many of the majors available on most campuses. It will provide you with a profile that you can compare with those of your fellow students. And, most important, it will produce some preliminary data that you can take to your college counselor.

Enjoy building your profile—and good luck in making your selection.

PART 1: YOUR PREFERENCES

Each of the following three pages lists twenty-four different statements. On each page, rate each statement by circling the appropriate number. Follow these rules:

- A 5 indicates you would look forward to the experience with maximum interest and enthusiasm.

- A 4 rating indicates high interest. You would get excited about such a learning experience.

- A 3 indicates moderate interest.

- A 2 signals only slight interest.

- A 1 says you would prefer not to participate at all.

This is a game or exercise, *not* a test. Work quickly—your first impressions will probably give the best results.

Have fun!

COLLEGE MAJORS (1)

1. Preparing for a wide variety of career opportunities in health services.　　5　4　3　2　1

2. Wearing a uniform that denotes authority.　　5　4　3　2　1

3. Dealing with financial figures and forms.　　5　4　3　2　1

4. Working with youth; having long summer vacations.　　5　4　3　2　1

5. Taking courses in the humanities.　　5　4　3　2　1

6. Working with mathematics, materials, and designs.　　5　4　3　2　1

7. Writing, painting, dancing, singing, performing professionally.　　5　4　3　2　1

8. Getting on the track leading to science and high tech careers.　　5　4　3　2　1

9. Becoming a communication specialist.　　5　4　3　2　1

10. Reaching an executive level.　　5　4　3　2　1

11. Thinking about the meaning of life.　　5　4　3　2　1

12. Speaking with eloquence.　　5　4　3　2　1

13. Engaging in public relations.　　5　4　3　2　1

14. Developing your interest in improving the environment.　　5　4　3　2　1

15. Becoming a foreign exchange student.　　5　4　3　2　1

16. Seeking knowledge from early cultures.　　5　4　3　2　1

17. Investigating the many forms of advanced technology.　　5　4　3　2　1

18. Becoming an expert in data processing.　　5　4　3　2　1

19. Trying to find out how a business system works.　　5　4　3　2　1

20. Reading biographies of ancient leaders.　　5　4　3　2　1

21. Preparing for a life in politics.　　5　4　3　2　1

22. Wanting to know what makes people tick.　　5　4　3　2　1

23. Evaluating the behavior of people in groups.　　5　4　3　2　1

24. Preparing to be a city manager or other government official.　　5　4　3　2　1

COLLEGE MAJORS (2)

		Scale				
1.	Wanting to help others.	5	4	3	2	1
2.	Learning about firearms and court systems.	5	4	3	2	1
3.	Working with computers and spreadsheets.	5	4	3	2	1
4.	Helping youth reach their potential.	5	4	3	2	1
5.	Achieving a broad cultural background.	5	4	3	2	1
6.	Building complex structures and machines.	5	4	3	2	1
7.	Working with artistic materials, doing interiors, making life more beautiful.	5	4	3	2	1
8.	Solving and using mathematical formulas.	5	4	3	2	1
9.	Developing your interest in comparative literature, great novels, poetry.	5	4	3	2	1
10.	Becoming a business leader.	5	4	3	2	1
11.	Comparing religions.	5	4	3	2	1
12.	Converting a variety of communication courses into a career.	5	4	3	2	1
13.	Being intrigued with all aspects of the media and advertising.	5	4	3	2	1
14.	Preparing for research involving living creatures.	5	4	3	2	1
15.	Becoming an interpreter.	5	4	3	2	1
16.	Taking field trips; doing ''digs.''	5	4	3	2	1
17.	Working in a high-tech environment.	5	4	3	2	1
18.	Learning about computer technology.	5	4	3	2	1
19.	Knowing how the law of supply and demand works.	5	4	3	2	1
20.	Visiting museums.	5	4	3	2	1
21.	Knowing the political process.	5	4	3	2	1
22.	Studying the behavior of others; learning to know more about yourself.	5	4	3	2	1
23.	Analyzing the behavior of people of all ages and ethnic backgrounds.	5	4	3	2	1
24.	Running a government agency.	5	4	3	2	1

COLLEGE MAJORS (3)

Scale

1. Taking science courses to qualify for people-oriented careers.   5   4   3   2   1

2. Devoting your life to protecting others.   5   4   3   2   1

3. Communicating financial goals through statistical graphics.   5   4   3   2   1

4. Enjoying the learning process.   5   4   3   2   1

5. Enjoying subjects that are not career directed.   5   4   3   2   1

6. Creating technical prototypes.   5   4   3   2   1

7. Becoming involved in the artistic world.   5   4   3   2   1

8. Working with numbers more than words.   5   4   3   2   1

9. Working with words more than numbers.   5   4   3   2   1

10. Seeking and administering ways in which to motivate others to produce.   5   4   3   2   1

11. Exploring life through a study of the works of the masters.   5   4   3   2   1

12. Giving talks in front of large groups.   5   4   3   2   1

13. Promoting products or services.   5   4   3   2   1

14. Studying earth and marine sciences.   5   4   3   2   1

15. Speaking to others in their language, not yours.   5   4   3   2   1

16. Helping people understand themselves through a study of past cultures.   5   4   3   2   1

17. Combining mathematics, materials, and technical skills.   5   4   3   2   1

18. Parlaying computer skills and knowledge into success.   5   4   3   2   1

19. Charting business cycles; dealing in foreign exchange currencies.   5   4   3   2   1

20. Converting a study of the past into a better understanding of the present.   5   4   3   2   1

21. Running for political office.   5   4   3   2   1

22. Taking the clinical approach to human behavior.   5   4   3   2   1

23. Looking into people's lifestyle characteristics.   5   4   3   2   1

24. Taking business management courses in order to operate public organizations.   5   4   3   2   1

PART 2: YOUR PROFILE

Now that you have indicated your preferences, enjoy building your personal profile. The results will indicate those college majors you should explore further.

Step 1: Study the profile sheet on the next page.

- Notice that there are twenty-four college major possibilities across the top. Your campus may offer a different list with different titles. If so, have your college counselor assist you in making adjustments.

- There is space (number 25) for a major you prefer over those listed. Examples include Agriculture, Forestry, Home Economics, Geography. If your preferred major is not listed, write it in, rate it on the scale, and make comparisons.

- The scale on the left side measures high, medium, and low interest in each major.

- A space is provided across the bottom for you to enter the total for each major.

Step 2: Total the numbers you circled for question 1 on each of the three previous pages. Enter this total (it will be between 3 and 15) at the bottom of column 1 (Health Services).

Step 3: Total the numbers for question 2 and enter it at the bottom of column 2 (Criminal Justice). Continue until you have entered the total at the bottom of each of the twenty-four columns.

Step 4: On the scale at the left (0 to 15), locate the level equal to your total in each column. Place a dot at the level of your total for each column. Connect these dots and you have your profile.

Step 5: Indicate your top three choices with a star or other distinctive mark. You will want to research these three possibilities first.

PROFILE SHEET

COLLEGE MAJORS

	HEALTH SERVICES	CRIMINAL JUSTICE	ACCOUNTING	EDUCATION	LIBERAL ARTS	ENGINEERING	FINE ARTS	MATHEMATICS	ENGLISH	MANAGEMENT	PHILOSOPHY	COMMUNICATIONS	MARKETING	NATURAL SCIENCES	FOREIGN LANGUAGE	ANTHROPOLOGY	TECHNOLOGY	COMPUTER SCIENCE	ECONOMICS	HISTORY	POLITICAL SCIENCE	PSYCHOLOGY	SOCIOLOGY	PUBLIC ADMINISTRATION	OTHER
15																									
HIGH																									
10																									
MEDIUM																									
5																									
LOW																									
0																									
Question Numbers	1	2	3	4	5	6	7	8	9	10	11	12	13	14	15	16	17	18	19	20	21	22	23	24	25

Write in the totals for each question on all three pages.

PART 3: EVALUATION

It is now time to evaluate your profile. Like your personality, it is uniquely yours and should be studied carefully. Here are some tips that will help you make your interpretation:

- Match your profile with that of another student. Significant insights can be uncovered through the comparison process.

- Keep in mind that different majors can follow the same academic track at the beginning.

- Investigate *all* of your high-interest choices. One way to do this is to talk with professors who teach in these areas. Also check the college catalog for appropriate courses. Study career opportunities and organizations related to the major. Spend time in a career center looking over pamphlets and monographs that will provide you with details on where a major will lead you.

As stated previously, each campus has not only developed its own academic majors but different titles can be assigned to the same major. *Please see your academic counselor for local adjustments.* She or he can assist you in matching your choices with the curriculum on your campus.

NOTES

NOTES

OVER 150 BOOKS AND 35 VIDEOS AVAILABLE IN THE 50-MINUTE SERIES

We hope you enjoyed this book. If so, we have good news for you. This title is part of the best-selling *50-MINUTE*™ *Series* of books. All *Series* books are similar in size and identical in price. Many are supported with training videos.

To order *50-MINUTE* Books and Videos or request a free catalog, contact your local distributor or Crisp Publications, Inc., 1200 Hamilton Court, Menlo Park, CA 94025. Our toll-free number is (800) 442-7477.

50-Minute Series Books and Videos Subject Areas . . .

Management
Training
Human Resources
Customer Service and Sales Training
Communications
Small Business and Financial Planning
Creativity
Personal Development
Wellness
Adult Literacy and Learning
Career, Retirement and Life Planning

Other titles available from Crisp Publications in these categories

Crisp Computer Series
The Crisp Small Business & Entrepreneurship Series
Quick Read Series
Management
Personal Development
Retirement Planning